The Society of the Spectacle

Translated by Donald Nicholson-Smith

The Society of the Spectacle

Guy Debord

ZONE BOOKS · NEW YORK

1995

Translation © 1994 Donald Nicholson-Smith
ZONE BOOKS
611 Broadway, Suite 608
New York, NY 10012

*First Paperback Edition
Fifth Printing 1999*

Originally published in France as *La société du spectacle*.
in 1967 by Buchet-Chastel. This English language
translation published by arrangement with Editions
Gallimard © 1992.

Printed in the United States of America

Distributed by The MIT Press,
Cambridge, Massachusetts, and London, England

Library of Congress Cataloging-in-Publication Data

Debord, Guy, 1931–
    [La société du spectacle. English]
    The Society of the Spectacle / by Guy Debord
    p.   cm.
    Translation of: La société du spectacle.
    ISBN 0-942299-79-5
    1. Social psychology. 2. Proletariat. 3. Social
classes. I. Title.
HN291.D413   1990
302–dc20   89-39940
                                           CIP

Contents

Translator's Acknowledgements

I am most grateful to Evelyne Chasse, Robert Chasse, Tim Clark and Bruce Elwell for the benefit of their advice on many points of translation. I am also greatly indebted to Mia Nadezhda Rublowska for all her help.

I should like to dedicate the translation to the memory of a true friend of this book, Fredy Perlman, who, with a handful of comrades, published it in English for the first time, and kept it in print for more than twenty years.

Donald Nicholson-Smith   "Sero sed serio"
Brooklyn, 1993

Preface to the

Third French Edition

La Société du spectacle was first published in November
1967 by the Paris publishers Buchet-Chastel. The disturb-
ances of 1968 made the book known. A second edition,
strictly unaltered, was issued in 1971 by Editions Champ
Libre, a publishing house whose name was changed to Editions Gérard Lebovici in 1984 in the wake of the murder
of the publisher. That edition was reprinted regularly until
1991. The text of this third edition is also identical to that
of 1967. (Naturally, the same principle will be applied to
my other books, all of which are to be republished by
Gallimard; I am not someone who revises his work.)

A critical theory of the kind presented here needed no
changing — not as long, at any rate, as the general conditions of the long historical period that it was the first to
describe accurately were still intact. The continued unfolding of our epoch has merely confirmed and further
illustrated the theory of the spectacle. The reiteration of
this theory may also be considered historical in a less ele-
vated sense, for it testifies to what was the most extreme

position taken up during the confrontations of 1968, and hence to what it was possible to know by then. The biggest dupes of that time have since received a clear object lesson – in the form of their own shattered existences – as to what exactly was meant by the "negation of life become visible," by the "loss of quality" associated with the commodity-form or by the "proletarianization of the world."

I have since – as called for – added postscripts on the more striking novelties thrown up by the fundamental movement of the times. In 1979, in the preface to a new Italian translation, I dealt with the effective changes in the nature of industrial production, as in the techniques of government, that began with the deployment of the power of the spectacle. And in 1988 my *Comments on the Society of the Spectacle* offered irrefutable evidence that the former "worldwide division of spectacular tasks" between the rival realms of the "concentrated" and "diffuse" forms of the spectacle had now given way to a combined form – to an "integrated" spectacle.

This amalgamation might be summed up by slightly revising Thesis 105 of *The Society of the Spectacle*, which drew a distinction, on the basis of the situation prior to 1967, between two different forms of practice: the Great Schism of class power having been reconciled, we ought now to say that the unified practice of the integrated spectacle has "transformed the world economically" *as well as* "using police methods to transform perception." (The police in question, incidentally, are of a completely new variety.)

It was only because this fusion had already occurred worldwide on the economic and political planes that the

8

world could be declared officially unified. It was, further-more, only because of the grave predicament in which separated power universally finds itself that this world needed unifying post haste, so that it might function as *one bloc* in a single consensual organization of the world market, at once travestied and buttressed by the spectacle. And yet, in the end, it will not be unified.

The totalitarian bureaucracy – that "substitute ruling class for the market economy" – never had much faith in its own destiny. It knew itself to be nothing but an "undeveloped type of ruling class" even as it yearned to be something more. Long ago, Thesis 58 had established as axiomatic that "The spectacle has its roots in the fertile field of the economy, and it is the produce of this field which must in the end come to dominate the spectacular market."

This striving of the spectacle toward modernization and unification, together with all the other tendencies toward the simplification of society, was what in 1989 led the Russian bureaucracy suddenly, and as one man, to convert to the current *ideology* of democracy – in other words, to the dictatorial freedom of the Market, as tempered by the recognition of the rights of Homo Spectator. No one in the West felt the need to spend more than a single day considering the import and impact of this extraordinary media event – proof enough, were proof called for, of the progress made by the techniques of the spectacle. All that needed recording was the fact that a sort of geological tremor had apparently taken place. The phenomenon was duly noted, dated and deemed sufficiently well under-

9

stood; a very simple sign, "the fall of the Berlin Wall," repeated over and over again, immediately attained the incontestability of all the other *signs of democracy*.

In 1991 the first effects of this spectacular moderniza- tion were felt in the complete disintegration of Russia. Thus – more clearly even than in the West – were the dis- astrous results of the general development of the economy made manifest. The disorder presently reigning in the East is no more than a consequence. The same formidable ques- tion that has been haunting the world for two centuries is about to be posed again *everywhere*: How can the poor be made to work once their illusions have been shattered, and once force has been defeated?

Thesis 111, discerning the first symptoms of that Rus- sian decline whose final explosion we have just witnessed and envisioning the early disappearance of a world soci- ety which (as we may now put it) will one day be erased from the memory of the computer, offered a strategic assessment whose accuracy will very soon be obvious: The "crumbling of the worldwide alliance founded on bureaucratic mystification is in the last analysis the most unfavorable portent for the future development of capital- ist society."

This book should be read bearing in mind that it was written with the deliberate intention of doing harm to spectacular society. There was never anything outrageous, however, about what it had to say.

Guy Debord
June 30, 1992

I

Separation Perfected

But certainly for the present age, which prefers the sign to the thing signified, the copy to the original, representation to reality, the appearance to the essence... illusion only is sacred, truth *profane. Nay, sacredness is held to be enhanced in proportion as truth decreases and illusion increases, so that the highest degree of illusion comes to be the highest degree of sacredness.*
– Feuerbach, Preface to the second edition of *The Essence of Christianity*

1   THE WHOLE LIFE of those societies in which modern conditions of production prevail presents itself as an immense

accumulation of *spectacles*. All that once was directly lived
has become mere representation.

2   IMAGES DETACHED FROM every aspect of life merge into
a common stream, and the former unity of life is lost forever. Apprehended in a *partial* way, reality unfolds in a new
generality as a pseudo-world apart, solely as an object of
contemplation. The tendency toward the specialization of
images-of-the-world finds its highest expression in the
world of the autonomous image, where deceit deceives
itself. The spectacle in its generality is a concrete inversion of life, and, as such, the autonomous movement of
non-life.

3   THE SPECTACLE APPEARS at once as society itself, as a
part of society and as a means of unification. As a part of
society, it is that sector where all attention, all consciousness, converges. Being isolated — and precisely for that
reason — this sector is the locus of illusion and false consciousness; the unity it imposes is merely the official language of generalized separation.

4   THE SPECTACLE IS NOT a collection of images; rather, it
is a social relationship between people that is mediated
by images.

5   THE SPECTACLE CANNOT be understood either as a deliberate distortion of the visual world or as a product of the

12

technology of the mass dissemination of images. It is far better viewed as a weltanschauung that has been actualized, translated into the material realm — a world view transformed into an objective force.

6   UNDERSTOOD IN ITS TOTALITY, the spectacle is both the outcome and the goal of the dominant mode of production. It is not something *added* to the real world — not a decorative element, so to speak. On the contrary, it is the very heart of society's real unreality. In all its specific manifestations — news or propaganda, advertising or the actual consumption of entertainment — the spectacle epitomizes the prevailing model of social life. It is the omnipresent celebration of a choice *already made* in the sphere of production, and the consummate result of that choice. In form as in content the spectacle serves as total justification for the conditions and aims of the existing system. It further ensures the *permanent presence* of that justification, for it governs almost all time spent outside the production process itself.

7   THE PHENOMENON OF SEPARATION is part and parcel of the unity of the world, of a global social praxis that has split up into reality on the one hand and image on the other. Social practice, which the spectacle's autonomy challenges, is also the real totality to which the spectacle is subordinate. So deep is the rift in this totality, however, that the spectacle is able to emerge as its apparent goal. The language of the spectacle is composed of *signs* of the dominant organization of production — signs which are at the same time the ultimate end-products of that organization.

13

8   THE SPECTACLE CANNOT be set in abstract opposition to
concrete social activity, for the dichotomy between reality and image will survive on either side of any such distinction. Thus the spectacle, though it turns reality on its
head, is itself a product of real activity. Likewise, lived reality suffers the material assaults of the spectacle's mechanisms of contemplation, incorporating the spectacular
order and lending that order positive support. Each side
therefore has its share of objective reality. And every concept, as it takes its place on one side or the other, has no
foundation apart from its transformation into its opposite:
reality erupts within the spectacle, and the spectacle is
real. This reciprocal alienation is the essence and under-
pinning of society as it exists.

 9   IN A WORLD THAT *really* has been turned on its head,
truth is a moment of falsehood.

10   THE CONCEPT OF the spectacle brings together and ex-
plains a wide range of apparently disparate phenomena.
Diversities and contrasts among such phenomena are the
appearances of the spectacle – the appearances of a social
organization of appearances that needs to be grasped in its
general truth. Understood on its own terms, the spectacle proclaims the predominance of appearances and asserts
that all human life, which is to say all social life, is mere
appearance. But any critique capable of apprehending the
spectacle's essential character must expose it as a visible
negation of life – and as a negation of life that has *invented
a visual form for itself.*

11 IN ORDER TO DESCRIBE the spectacle, its formation, its
functions and whatever forces may hasten its demise, a few
artificial distinctions are called for. To analyze the spectacle means talking its language to some degree — to the
degree, in fact, that we are obliged to engage the methodology of the society to which the spectacle gives expression. For what the spectacle expresses is the total practice
of one particular economic and social formation; it is, so
to speak, that formation's *agenda*. It is also the historical
moment by which we happen to be governed.

12 THE SPECTACLE MANIFESTS itself as an enormous positiv-
ity, out of reach and beyond dispute. All it says is: "Everything that appears is good; whatever is good will appear."
The attitude that it demands in principle is the same passive acceptance that it has already secured by means of its
seeming incontrovertibility, and indeed by its monopolization of the realm of appearances.

13 THE SPECTACLE IS essentially tautological, for the simple
reason that its means and its ends are identical. It is the
sun that never sets on the empire of modern passivity. It
covers the entire globe, basking in the perpetual warmth
of its own glory.

14 THE SPECTACULAR CHARACTER of modern industrial
society has nothing fortuitous or superficial about it; on
the contrary, this society is based on the spectacle in the
most fundamental way. For the spectacle, as the perfect
image of the ruling economic order, ends are nothing and

15

development is all — although the only thing into which the spectacle plans to develop is itself.

15 AS THE INDISPENSABLE PACKAGING for things produced as they are now produced, as a general gloss on the rationality of the system, and as the advanced economic sector directly responsible for the manufacture of an ever-growing mass of image-objects, the spectacle is the *chief product* of present-day society.

16 THE SPECTACLE SUBJECTS living human beings to its will to the extent that the economy has brought them under its sway. For the spectacle is simply the economic realm developing *for itself* — at once a faithful mirror held up to the production of things and a distorting objectification of the producers.

17 AN EARLIER STAGE in the economy's domination of social life entailed an obvious downgrading of *being* into *having* that left its stamp on all human endeavor. The present stage, in which social life is completely taken over by the accumulated products of the economy, entails a generalized shift from *having* to appearing: all effective "having" must now derive both its immediate prestige and its ultimate raison d'être from appearances. At the same time all individual reality, being directly dependent on social power and completely shaped by that power, has assumed a social character. Indeed, it is only inasmuch as individual reality *is not* that it is allowed to *appear*.

18   FOR ONE TO WHOM the real world becomes real images,
mere images are transformed into real beings – tangible
figments which are the efficient motor of trancelike behavior. Since the spectacle's job is to cause a world that is no
longer directly perceptible to be *seen* via different specialized mediations, it is inevitable that it should elevate the
human sense of sight to the special place once occupied
by touch; the most abstract of the senses, and the most
easily deceived, sight is naturally the most readily adapta-
ble to present-day society's generalized abstraction. This
is not to say, however, that the spectacle itself is perceptible to the naked eye – even if that eye is assisted by the
ear. The spectacle is by definition immune from human
activity, inaccessible to any projected review or correction.
It is the opposite of dialogue. Wherever representation
takes on an independent existence, the spectacle reestab-
lishes its rule.

19   THE SPECTACLE IS HEIR to all the weakness of the project
of Western philosophy, which was an attempt to understand activity by means of the categories of vision. Indeed
the spectacle reposes on an incessant deployment of the
very technical rationality to which that philosophical tradition gave rise. So far from realizing philosophy, the spectacle philosophizes reality, and turns the material life of
everyone into a universe of speculation.

20   PHILOSOPHY IS AT ONCE the power of alienated thought
and the thought of alienated power, and as such it has never
been able to emancipate itself from theology. The specta-

17

cle is the material reconstruction of the religious illusion. Not that its techniques have dispelled those religious mists in which human beings once located their own powers, the very powers that had been wrenched from them – but those cloud-enshrouded entities have now been brought down to earth. It is thus the most earthbound aspects of life that have become the most impenetrable and rarefied. The absolute denial of life, in the shape of a fallacious paradise, is no longer projected onto the heavens, but finds its place instead within material life itself. The spectacle is hence a technological version of the exiling of human powers in a "world beyond" – and the perfection of separation *within* human beings.

21　SO LONG AS THE REALM of necessity remains a social dream, dreaming will remain a social necessity. The spectacle is the bad dream of modern society in chains, expressing nothing more than its wish for sleep. The spectacle is the guardian of that sleep.

22　THE FACT THAT the practical power of modern society has detached itself from itself and established itself in the spectacle as an independent realm can only be explained by the self-cleavage and self-contradictoriness already present in that powerful practice.

23　AT THE ROOT OF the spectacle lies that oldest of all social divisions of labor, the specialization of *power*. The specialized role played by the spectacle is that of spokesman for all other activities, a sort of diplomatic representative of hierarchical society at its own court, and the source of the only discourse which that society allows itself to hear. Thus the most modern aspect of the spectacle is also at bottom the most archaic.

24 BY MEANS OF THE SPECTACLE the ruling order discourses endlessly upon itself in an uninterrupted monologue of self-praise. The spectacle is the self-portrait of power in the age of power's totalitarian rule over the conditions of existence. The fetishistic appearance of pure objectivity in spectacular relationships conceals their true character as relationships between human beings and between classes; a second Nature thus seems to impose inescapable laws upon our environment. But the spectacle is by no means the inevitable outcome of a technical development perceived as *natural*; on the contrary, the society of the spectacle is a form that chooses its own technical content. If the spectacle — understood in the limited sense of those "mass media" that are its most stultifying superficial manifestation — seems at times to be invading society in the shape of a mere *apparatus*, it should be remembered that this apparatus has nothing neutral about it, and that it answers precisely to the needs of the spectacle's internal dynamics. If the social requirements of the age which develops such techniques can be met only through their mediation, if the administration of society and all contact between people now depends on the intervention of such "instant" communication, it is because this "communication" is essentially *one-way*; the concentration of the media thus amounts to the monopolization by the admin-

istrators of the existing system of the means to pursue their particular form of administration. The social cleavage that the spectacle expresses is inseparable from the modern State, which, as the product of the social division of labor and the organ of class rule, is the general form of all social division.

25 SEPARATION IS THE alpha and omega of the spectacle. Religious contemplation in its earliest form was the outcome of the establishment of the social division of labor and the formation of classes. Power draped itself in the outward garb of a mythical order from the beginning. In former times the category of the sacred justified the cosmic and ontological ordering of things that best served the interests of the masters, expounding upon and embellishing what society *could not deliver*. Thus power as a separate realm has always had a spectacular aspect, but mass allegiance to frozen religious imagery was originally a shared acknowledgment of loss, an imaginary compensation for a poverty of real social activity that was still widely felt to be a universal fact of life. The modern spectacle, by contrast, depicts what society *can deliver*, but within this depiction what is permitted is rigidly distinguished from what is possible. The spectacle preserves unconsciousness as practical changes in the conditions of existence proceed. The spectacle is self-generated, and it makes up its own rules: it is a specious form of the sacred. And it makes no secret of what it *is*, namely, hierarchical power evolving on its own, in its separateness, thanks to an increasing productivity based on an ever more refined division of labor,

an ever greater comminution of machine-governed g
tures, and an ever-widening market. In the course of t
development all community and critical awareness have
ceased to be; nor have those forces, which were able – by
separating – to grow enormously in strength, yet found a
way to *reunite*.

26 THE GENERALIZED SEPARATION of worker and product
has spelled the end of any comprehensive view of the job
done, as well as the end of direct personal communication
between producers. As the accumulation of alienated products proceeds, and as the productive process gets more
concentrated, consistency and communication become the
exclusive assets of the system's managers. The triumph of
an economic system founded on separation leads to the
proletarianization of the world.

27 OWING TO THE VERY success of this separated system of
production, whose product is separation itself, that fundamental area of experience which was associated in earlier societies with an individual's principal work is being
transformed – at least at the leading edge of the system's
evolution – into a realm of non-work, of inactivity. Such
inactivity, however, is by no means emancipated from productive activity: it remains in thrall to that activity, in an
uneasy and worshipful subjection to production's needs
and results; indeed it is itself a product of the rationality
of production. There can be no freedom apart from activity, and within the spectacle all activity is banned – a corollary of the fact that all *real* activity has been forcibly

21

channeled into the global construction of the spectacle. So what is referred to as "liberation from work," that is, increased leisure time, is a liberation neither within labor itself nor from the world labor has brought into being.

28 THE REIGNING ECONOMIC system is founded on isolation; at the same time it is a circular process designed to produce isolation. Isolation underpins technology, and technology isolates in its turn; all *goods* proposed by the spectacular system, from cars to televisions, also serve as weapons for that system as it strives to reinforce the isolation of "the lonely crowd." The spectacle is continually rediscovering its own basic assumptions – and each time in a more concrete manner.

29 THE ORIGIN OF THE spectacle lies in the world's loss of unity, and its massive expansion in the modern period demonstrates how total this loss has been: the abstract nature of all individual work, as of production in general, finds perfect expression in the spectacle, whose very *manner of being concrete* is, precisely, abstraction. The spectacle divides the world into two parts, one of which is held up as a self-representation to the world, and is superior to the world. The spectacle is simply the common language that bridges this division. Spectators are linked only by a one-way relationship to the very center that maintains their isolation from one another. The spectacle thus unites what is separate, but it unites it only *in its separateness*.

30   THE SPECTATOR'S ALIENATION from and submission to the contemplated object (which is the outcome of his unthinking activity) works like this: the more he contemplates, the less he lives; the more readily he recognizes his own needs in the images of need proposed by the dominant system, the less he understands his own existence and his own desires. The spectacle's externality with respect to the acting subject is demonstrated by the fact that the individual's own gestures are no longer his own, but rather those of someone else who represents them to him. The spectator feels at home nowhere, for the spectacle is everywhere.

31   WORKERS DO NOT produce themselves: they produce a force independent of themselves. The *success* of this production, that is, the abundance it generates, is experienced by its producers only as an *abundance of dispossession*. All time, all space, becomes *foreign* to them as their own alienated products accumulate. The spectacle is a map of this new world — a map drawn to the scale of the territory itself. In this way the very powers that have been snatched from us reveal themselves to us in their full force.

32   THE SPECTACLE'S FUNCTION in society is the concrete manufacture of alienation. Economic growth corresponds almost entirely to the growth of this particular sector of industrial production. If something *grows* along with the self-movement of the economy, it can only be the alienation that has inhabited the core of the economic sphere from its inception.

23

33 THOUGH SEPARATED FROM his product, man is more and more, and ever more powerfully, the producer of every detail of his world. The closer his life comes to being his own creation, the more drastically is he cut off from that life.

34 THE SPECTACLE IS *capital* accumulated to the point where it becomes image.

II

The Commodity as Spectacle

The commodity can only be understood in its undistorted essence when it becomes the universal category of society as a whole. Only in this context does the reification produced by commodity relations assume decisive importance both for the objective evolution of society and for the stance adopted by men towards it. Only then does the commodity become crucial for the subjugation of men's consciousness to the forms in which this reification finds expression.... As labor is progressively rationalized and mechanized man's lack of will is reinforced by the way in which his activity becomes less and less active and more and more contemplative.

– Lukács, *History and Class Consciousness*

35 THE SELF-MOVEMENT of the spectacle consists in this: it arrogates to itself everything that in human activity exists in a fluid state so as to possess it in a congealed form – as things that, being the *negative expression* of living value, have become exclusively abstract value. In these signs we recognize our old enemy the commodity, which appears at first sight a very trivial thing, and easily understood, yet which is in reality a very queer thing, abounding in metaphysical subtleties.

36 HERE WE HAVE the principle of commodity fetishism, the domination of society by things whose qualities are "at the same time perceptible and imperceptible by the senses." This principle is absolutely fulfilled in the spectacle, where the perceptible world is replaced by a set of images that are superior to that world yet at the same time impose themselves as *eminently* perceptible.

37 THE WORLD THE SPECTACLE holds up to view is at once *here* and *elsewhere*; it is the world of the commodity ruling over all lived experience. The commodity world is thus shown *as it really is*, for its logic is one with men's estrangement from one another and from the sum total of what they produce.

38 THE LOSS OF QUALITY so obvious at every level of the language of the spectacle, from the objects it lauds to the behavior it regulates, merely echoes the basic traits of a real production process that shuns reality. The commodity form is characterized exclusively by self-equivalence –

26

Quantity = superiority

it is exclusively quantitative in nature: the quantitative is what it develops, and it can only develop within the quantitative.

39   DESPITE THE FACT that it excludes quality, this development is still subject, qua development, to the qualitative. Thus the spectacle betrays the fact that it must eventually break the bounds of its own abundance. Though this is not true locally, except here and there, it is already true at the universal level which was the commodity's original standard – a standard that it has been able to live up to by turning the whole planet into a single world market.

40   THE DEVELOPMENT of the forces of production is the *real unconscious history* that has built and modified the conditions of existence of human groups (understood as the conditions of *survival* and their extension): this development has been the basis of all human enterprise. The realm of commodities has meant the constitution, within a natural economy, of a surplus survival. The production of commodities, which implies the exchange of a variety of products among independent producers, was long able to retain an artisanal aspect embodied in a marginal economic activity where its quantitative essence was masked. Wherever it encountered the social conditions of large-scale trade and capital accumulation, however, such production successfully established total hegemony over the economy. The entire economy then became what the commodity, throughout this campaign of conquest, had shown itself to be – namely, a process of quantitative development. The

27

unceasing deployment of economic power in the shape of commodities has transfigured human labor into labor-as-commodity, into wage-labor, and eventually given rise to an *abundance* thanks to which the basic problem of survival, though solved, is solved in such a way that it is not disposed of, but is rather forever cropping up again at a higher level. Economic growth liberates societies from the natural pressures occasioned by their struggle for survival, but they still must be liberated from their liberators. The *independence* of the commodity has spread to the entire economy over which the commodity now reigns. The economy transforms the world, but it transforms it into a world of the economy. The pseudo-nature in which labor has become alienated demands that such labor remain in its service indefinitely, and inasmuch as this estranged activity is answerable only to itself it is able in turn to enroll all socially permissible efforts and projects under its banner. In these circumstances an abundance of commodities, which is to say an abundance of commodity relations, can be no more than an *augmented survival*.

41 THE COMMODITY'S DOMINION over the economy was at first exercised in a covert manner. The economy itself, the material basis of social life, was neither perceived nor understood – not properly known precisely because of its "familiarity." In a society where concrete commodities were few and far between, it was the dominance of money that seemed to play the role of emissary, invested with full authority by an unknown power. With the coming of the industrial revolution, the division of labor specific to that

revolution's manufacturing system, and mass production for a world market, the commodity emerged in its full-fledged form as a force aspiring to the complete colonization of social life. It was at this moment too that political economy established itself as at once the dominant science and the science of domination.

42   THE SPECTACLE CORRESPONDS to the historical moment at which the commodity completes its colonization of social life. It is not just that the relationship to commodities is now plain to see — commodities are now *all* that there is to see; the world we see is the world of the commodity. The growth of the dictatorship of modern economic production is both extensive and intensive in character. In the least industrialized regions its presence is already felt in the form of imperialist domination by those areas that lead the world in productivity. In these advanced sectors themselves, social space is continually being blanketed by stratum after stratum of commodities. With the advent of the so-called second industrial revolution, alienated consumption is added to alienated production as an inescapable duty of the masses. The *entirety of labor sold* is transformed overall into the *total commodity*. A cycle is thus set in train that must be maintained at all costs: the total commodity must be returned in fragmentary form to a fragmentary individual completely cut off from the concerted action of the forces of production. To this end the already specialized science of domination is further broken down into specialties such as sociology, applied psychology, cybernetics, semiology and so

on, which oversee the self-regulation of every phase of the process.

43 WHEREAS AT THE PRIMITIVE stage of capitalist accumulation "political economy treats the *proletarian* as a mere *worker*" who must receive only the minimum necessary to guarantee his labor-power, and never considers him "in his leisure, in his humanity," these ideas of the ruling class are revised just as soon as so great an abundance of commodities begins to be produced that a surplus "collaboration" is required of the workers. All of a sudden the workers in question discover that they are no longer invariably subject to the total contempt so clearly built into every aspect of the organization and management of production; instead they find that every day, once work is over, they are treated like grown-ups, with a great show of solicitude and politeness, in their new role as consumers. The *humanity of the commodity* finally attends to the workers' "leisure and humanity" for the simple reason that political economy *as such* now can – and must – bring these spheres under its sway. Thus it is that the totality of human existence falls under the regime of the "perfected denial of man."

44 THE SPECTACLE IS a permanent opium war waged to make it impossible to distinguish goods from commodities, or true satisfaction from a survival that increases according to its own logic. Consumable survival *must* increase, in fact, because it continues to enshrine deprivation. The reason there is nothing *beyond* augmented survival, and no end to its growth, is that survival itself belongs to the realm

Utility is diminished

of dispossession: it may gild poverty, but it cannot transcend it.

45 AUTOMATION, WHICH IS at once the most advanced sector of modern industry and the epitome of its practice, confronts the world of the commodity with a contradiction that it must somehow resolve: the same technical infrastructure that is capable of abolishing labor must at the same time preserve labor as a commodity — and indeed as the sole generator of commodities. If automation, or for that matter any mechanisms, even less radical ones, that can increase productivity, are to be prevented from reducing socially necessary labor-time to an unacceptably low level, new forms of employment have to be created. A happy solution presents itself in the growth of the tertiary or service sector in response to the immense strain on the supply lines of the army responsible for distributing and hyping the commodities of the moment. The coincidence is neat: on the one hand, the system is faced with the necessity of reintegrating newly redundant labor; on the other, the very factitiousness of the needs associated with the commodities on offer calls out a whole battery of reserve forces.

46 EXCHANGE VALUE COULD only have arisen as the proxy of use value, but the victory it eventually won with its own weapons created the preconditions for its establishment as an autonomous power. By activating all human use value and monopolizing that value's fulfillment, exchange value eventually gained the upper hand. The process of exchange

became indistinguishable from any conceivable utility, thereby placing use value at its mercy. Starting out as the condottiere of use value, exchange value ended up waging a war that was entirely its own.

47   THE FALLING RATE of use value, which is a constant of the capitalist economy, gives rise to a new form of privation within the realm of augmented survival; this is not to say that this realm is emancipated from the old poverty: on the contrary, it requires the vast majority to take part as wage workers in the unending pursuit of its ends — a requirement to which, as everyone knows, one must either submit or die. It is the reality of this situation — the fact that, even in its most impoverished form (food, shelter), use value has no existence outside the illusory riches of augmented survival — that is the real basis for the general acceptance of illusion in the consumption of modern commodities. The real consumer thus becomes a consumer of illusion. The commodity is this illusion, which is in fact real, and the spectacle is its most general form.

48   USE VALUE WAS formerly implicit in exchange value. In terms of the spectacle's topsy-turvy logic, however, it has to be explicit — for the very reason that its own effective existence has been eroded by the overdevelopment of the commodity economy, and that a counterfeit life calls for a pseudo-justification.

49   THE SPECTACLE IS ANOTHER facet of money, which is the abstract general equivalent of all commodities. But

whereas money in its familiar form has dominated society as the representation of universal equivalence, that is, of the exchangeability of diverse goods whose uses are not otherwise compatible, the spectacle in its full development is money's modern aspect; in the spectacle the totality of the commodity world is visible in one piece, as the general equivalent of whatever society as a whole can be and do. The spectacle is money *for contemplation only*, for here the totality of use has already been bartered for the totality of abstract representation. The spectacle is not just the servant of *pseudo-use* — it is already, in itself, the pseudo-use of life.

50 WITH THE ACHIEVEMENT of a purely economic abundance, the concentrated result of social labor becomes visible, subjecting all reality to an appearance that is in effect that labor's product. Capital is no longer the invisible center determining the mode of production. As it accumulates, capital spreads out to the periphery, where it assumes the form of tangible objects. Society in its length and breadth becomes capital's faithful portrait.

51 THE ECONOMY'S TRIUMPH as an independent power inevitably also spells its doom, for it has unleashed forces that must eventually destroy the *economic necessity* that was the unchanging basis of earlier societies. Replacing that necessity by the necessity of boundless economic development can only mean replacing the satisfaction of primary human needs, now met in the most summary manner, by a ceaseless manufacture of pseudo-needs, all of which come down

in the end to just one – namely, the pseudo-need for the reign of an autonomous economy to continue. Such an economy irrevocably breaks all ties with authentic needs to the precise degree that it emerges from a *social unconscious* that was dependent on it without knowing it. "Whatever is conscious wears out. Whatever is unconscious remains unalterable. Once freed, however, surely this too must fall into ruins?" (Freud).

52 BY THE TIME society discovers that it is contingent on the economy, the economy has in point of fact become contingent on society. Having grown as a subterranean force until it could emerge sovereign, the economy proceeds to lose its power. Where economic id was, there ego shall be. The *subject* can only arise out of society – that is, out of the struggle that society embodies. The possibility of a subject's existing depends on the outcome of the class struggle which turns out to be the product and the producer of history's economic foundation.

53 "CONSCIOUSNESS OF DESIRE and the desire for consciousness together and indissolubly constitute that project which in its negative form has as its goal the abolition of classes and the direct possession by the workers of every aspect of their activity. The opposite of this project is the society of the spectacle, where the commodity contemplates itself in a world of its own making.

III

UNITY AND DIVISION
WITHIN APPEARANCES

A lively new polemic about the concepts "one divides into two" and "two fuse into one" is unfolding on the philosophical front in this country. This debate is a struggle between those who are for and those who are against the materialist dialectic, a struggle between two conceptions of the world: the proletarian conception and the bourgeois conception. Those who maintain that "one divides into two" is the fundamental law of things are on the side of the materialist dialectic; those who maintain that the fundamental law of things is that "two fuse into one" are against the materialist dialectic. The two sides have drawn a clear line of demarcation between them, and their arguments are diametrically opposed. This polemic is a reflection, on the ideological level, of the acute and complex class struggle taking place in China and in the world.

— *Red Flag* (Peking), 21 September 1964

54 LIKE MODERN SOCIETY itself, the spectacle is at once
united and divided. In both, unity is grounded in a split.
As it emerges in the spectacle, however, this contradiction
is itself contradicted by virtue of a reversal of its meaning:
division is presented as unity, and unity as division.

55 STRUGGLES BETWEEN FORCES, all of which have been
established for the purpose of running the same socioeco-
nomic system, are thus officially passed off as real antagonisms. In actuality these struggles partake of a real unity,
and this on the world stage as well as within each nation.

56 THIS IS NOT TO SAY that the spectacle's sham battles
between competing versions of alienated power are not
also real; they do express the system's uneven and conflict-
ridden development, as well as the relatively contradictory
interests of those classes or fractions of classes that recognize the system and strive in this way to carve out a role
for themselves in it. Just as the development of the most
advanced economies involves clashes between different
agendas, so totalitarian economic management by a state
bureaucracy and the condition of those countries living
under colonialism or semi-colonialism are likewise highly
differentiated with respect to modes of production and
power. By pointing up these great differences, while ap-
pealing to criteria of quite a different order, the spectacle
is able to portray them as markers of radically distinct
social systems. But from the standpoint of their actual reality as mere *sectors*, it is clear that the specificity of each is
subsumed under a universal system as functions of a sin-

gle tendency that has taken the planet for its field of operations. That tendency is capitalism.

57 THE SOCIETY THAT brings the spectacle into being does not dominate underdeveloped regions solely through the exercise of economic hegemony. It also dominates them in its capacity *as the society of the spectacle*. Modern society has thus already invested the social surface of every continent — even where the material basis of economic exploitation is still lacking — by spectacular means. It can frame the agenda of a ruling class and preside over that class's constitution. And, much as it proposes pseudogoods to be coveted, it may also offer false models of revolution to local revolutionaries. As for the bureaucratic power that rules in a number of industrialized countries, it certainly has its own peculiar spectacle, but this plays an integral part in the overarching spectacle as general pseudo-negation — and hence as vital support. So even if in its local manifestations the spectacle may embody totalitarian varieties of social communication and control, when viewed from the standpoint of the system's global functioning these are seen to be merely different aspects of a *worldwide division of spectacular tasks*.

58 THOUGH DESIGNED TO maintain the existing order as a whole, the division of spectacular tasks is chiefly oriented toward the actively developing pole of that order. The spectacle has its roots in the fertile field of the economy, and it is the produce of that field which must in the end come to dominate the spectacular market, whatever ide-

ological or police-state barriers of a protectionist kind may be set up by local spectacles with dreams of autarky.

59 BEHIND THE GLITTER of the spectacle's distractions, modern society lies in thrall to the global domination of a *banalizing* trend that also dominates it at each point where the most advanced forms of commodity consumption have seemingly broadened the panoply of roles and objects available to choose from. The vestiges of religion and of the family (still the chief mechanism for the passing on of class power), and thus too the vestiges of the moral repression that these institutions ensure, can now be seamlessly combined with the rhetorical advocacy of pleasure *in this life*. The life in question is after all produced solely as a form of pseudo-gratification which still embodies repression. A smug acceptance of what exists is likewise quite compatible with a purely spectacular rebelliousness, for the simple reason that dissatisfaction itself becomes a commodity as soon as the economics of affluence finds a way of applying its production methods to this particular raw material.

60 MEDIA STARS ARE SPECTACULAR representations of living human beings, distilling the essence of the spectacle's banality into images of possible roles. Stardom is a diversification in the semblance of life – the object of an identification with mere appearance which is intended to compensate for the crumbling of directly experienced diversifications of productive activity. Celebrities figure various styles of life and various views of society which anyone is supposedly free to embrace and pursue in a *global* man-

ner. Themselves incarnations of the inaccessible results of social labor, they mimic by-products of that labor, and project these above labor so that they appear as its goal. The by-products in question are *power* and *leisure* — the power to decide and the leisure to consume which are the alpha and the omega of a process that is never questioned. In the former case, government power assumes the personified form of the pseudo-star; in the second, stars of consumption canvas for votes as pseudo-power over life lived. But, just as none of these celestial activities are truly *global*, neither do they offer any real choices.

61   THE INDIVIDUAL WHO in the service of the spectacle is placed in stardom's spotlight is in fact the opposite of an individual, and as clearly the enemy of the individual in himself as of the individual in others. In entering the spectacle as a model to be identified with, he renounces all autonomy in order himself to identify with the general law of obedience to the course of things. Stars of consumption, though outwardly representing different personality types, actually show each of these types enjoying an equal access to the whole realm of consumption and deriving exactly the same satisfaction therefrom. Stars of decision, meanwhile, must possess the full range of accepted human qualities; all official differences between them are thus canceled out by the official *similarity* which is an inescapable implication of their supposed excellence in every sphere. Khrushchev had to become a general in order to have been responsible for the outcome of the battle of Kursk — not on the battlefield but twenty years later, as master of the

39

State. And Kennedy the orator survived himself, so to speak, and even delivered his own funeral oration, in the sense that Theodore Sorenson still wrote speeches for Kennedy's successor in the very style that had done so much to create the dead man's persona. The admirable people who personify the system are indeed well known for not being what they seem to be; they have achieved greatness by embracing a level of reality lower than that of the most insignificant individual life – and everyone knows it.

62 THE FALSE CHOICE offered by spectacular abundance, based on the juxtaposition, on the one hand, of competing yet mutually reinforcing spectacles and, on the other hand, of roles – for the most part signified by and embodied in objects – that are at once exclusive and interconnected, evolves into a contest among phantom qualities meant to elicit devotion to quantitative triviality. Thus false conflicts of ancient vintage tend to be resuscitated – regionalisms or racisms whose job it now is to invest vulgar rankings in the hierarchies of consumption with a magical ontological superiority. Hence too the never-ending succession of paltry contests – from competitive sports to elections – that are utterly incapable of arousing any truly *playful* feelings. Wherever the consumption of abundance has established itself, there is one spectacular antagonism which is always at the forefront of the range of illusory roles: the antagonism between youth and adulthood. For here an adult in the sense of someone who is master of his own life is nowhere to be found. And youth – implying change in what exists – is by no means proper to people

who are young. Rather, it characterizes only the economic system, the dynamism of capitalism: it is *things* that rule, that are young – things themselves that vie with each other and usurp one another's places.

63 WHAT SPECTACULAR ANTAGONISMS conceal is the *unity of poverty*. Differing forms of a single alienation contend in the masquerade of total freedom of choice by virtue of the fact that they are all founded on real repressed contradictions. Depending on the needs of the particular stage of poverty that it is supposed at once to deny and sustain, the spectacle may be *concentrated* or *diffuse* in form. In either case, it is no more than an image of harmony set amidst desolation and dread, at the still center of misfortune.

64 THE CONCENTRATED FORM of the spectacle normally characterizes bureaucratic capitalism, though it may on occasion be borrowed as a technique for buttressing state power over more backward mixed economies, and even the most advanced capitalism may call on it in moments of crisis. Bureaucratic property is itself concentrated, in that the individual bureaucrat's relation to the ownership of the economy as a whole is invariably mediated by the community of bureaucrats, by his membership in that community. And commodity production, less well developed in bureaucratic systems, is also concentrated in form: the commodity the bureaucracy appropriates is the totality of social labor, and what it sells back to society – *en bloc* – is society's survival. The dictatorship of the bureaucratic economy cannot leave the exploited masses any significant

margin of choice because it has had to make *all* the choices itself, and because any choice made independently of it, even the most trivial – concerning food, say, or music – amounts to a declaration of war to the death on the bureaucracy. This dictatorship must therefore be attended by permanent violence. Its spectacle imposes an image of the good which is a résumé of everything that exists officially, and this is usually concentrated in a single individual, the guarantor of the system's totalitarian cohesiveness. Everyone must identify magically with this absolute celebrity – or disappear. For this figure is the master of not-being-consumed, and the heroic image appropriate to the *absolute exploitation* constituted by primitive accumulation accelerated by terror. If every Chinese has to study Mao, and in effect *be* Mao, this is because there is *nothing else to be*. The dominion of the spectacle in its concentrated form means the dominion, too, of the police.

65   THE DIFFUSE FORM of the spectacle is associated with the abundance of commodities, with the undisturbed development of modern capitalism. Here each commodity considered in isolation is justified by an appeal to the grandeur of commodity production in general – a production for which the spectacle is an apologetic catalog. The claims jostling for position on the stage of the affluent economy's integrated spectacle are not always compatible, however. Similarly, different star commodities simultaneously promote conflicting approaches to the organization of society; thus the spectacular logic of the automobile argues for a perfect traffic flow entailing the destruction of the

old city centers, whereas the spectacle of the city itself calls for these same ancient sections to be turned into museums. So the already questionable satisfaction allegedly derived from the *consumption of the whole* is adulterated from the outset because the real consumer can only get his hands on a succession of *fragments* of this commodity heaven — fragments each of which naturally lacks any of the *quality* ascribed to the whole.

66 EACH INDIVIDUAL COMMODITY fights for itself, cannot acknowledge the others and aspires to impose its presence everywhere as though it were alone. The spectacle is the epic poem of this strife — a strife that no fall of Ilium can bring to an end. Of arms and the man the spectacle does not sing, but rather of passions and the commodity. Within this blind struggle each commodity, following where passion leads, unconsciously actualizes something of a higher order than itself: the commodity's becoming worldly coincides with the world's being transformed into commodities. So it is that, thanks to the cunning of the commodity, whereas all *particular* commodities wear themselves out in the fight, the commodity *as abstract form* continues on its way to absolute self-realization.

67 THE SATISFACTION THAT the commodity in its abundance can no longer supply by virtue of its use value is now sought in an acknowledgment of its value *qua commodity*. A use of the commodity arises that is sufficient unto itself; what this means for the consumer is an outpouring of religious zeal in honor of the commodity's sovereign freedom.

43

Waves of enthusiasm for particular products, fueled and boosted by the communications media, are propagated with lightning speed. A film sparks a fashion craze, or a magazine launches a chain of clubs that in turn spins off a line of products. The sheer fad item perfectly expresses the fact that, as the mass of commodities become more and more absurd, absurdity becomes a commodity in its own right. Keychains that are not paid for but come as free gifts with the purchase of some luxury product, or are then traded back and forth in a sphere far removed from that of their original use, bear eloquent witness to a mystical self-abandonment to the transcendent spirit of the commodity. Someone who collects keychains that have recently been manufactured for the sole purpose of being collected might be said to be accumulating the commodity's *indulgences* – the glorious tokens of the commodity's immanent presence among the faithful. In this way reified man proclaims his intimacy with the commodity. Following in the footsteps of the old religious fetishism, with its transported convulsionaries and miraculous cures, the fetishism of the commodity also achieves its moment of acute fervor. The only *use* still in evidence here, meanwhile, is the basic use of submission.

68   IT IS DOUBTLESS impossible to contrast the pseudo-need imposed by the reign of modern consumerism with any authentic need or desire that is not itself equally determined by society and its history. But the commodity in the stage of its abundance attests to an absolute break in the organic development of social needs. The commodi-

ty's mechanical accumulation unleashes a *limitless artificiality* in face of which all living desire is disarmed. The cumulative power of this autonomous realm of artifice necessarily everywhere entails a *falsification of life*.

69 THE IMAGE OF the blissful unification of society through consumption suspends disbelief with regard to the reality of division only until the next disillusionment occurs in the sphere of actual consumption. Each and every new product is supposed to offer a dramatic shortcut to the long-awaited promised land of total consumption. As such it is ceremoniously presented as the unique and ultimate product. But, as with the fashionable adoption of seemingly rare aristocratic first names which turn out in the end to be borne by a whole generation, so the would-be singularity of an object can be offered to the eager hordes only if it has been mass-produced. The sole real status attaching to a mediocre object of this kind is to have been placed, however briefly, at the very center of social life and hailed as the revelation of the goal of the production process. But even this spectacular prestige evaporates into vulgarity as soon as the object is taken home by a consumer – and hence by all other consumers too. At this point its essential poverty, the natural outcome of the poverty of its production, stands revealed – too late. For by this time another product will have been assigned to supply the system with its justification, and will in turn be demanding its moment of acclaim.

70 THIS CONTINUAL PROCESS of replacement means that fake gratification cannot help but be exposed as products

45

change, and as changes occur in the general conditions of production. Something that can assert its own unchanging excellence with uncontested arrogance changes nonetheless. This is as true of the concentrated as of the diffuse version of the spectacle, and only the *system* endures: Stalin, just like any obsolete product, can be cast aside by the very forces that promoted his rise. Each new lie of the advertising industry implicitly acknowledges the one before. Likewise every time a personification of totalitarian power is eclipsed, the illusion of community that has guaranteed that figure unanimous support is exposed as a mere sum of solitudes without illusions.

71 WHATEVER LAYS CLAIM to permanence in the spectacle is founded on change, and must change as that foundation changes. The spectacle, though quintessentially dogmatic, can yet produce no solid dogma. Nothing is stable for it: this is its natural state, albeit the state most at odds with its natural inclination.

72 THE UNREAL UNITY the spectacle proclaims masks the class division on which the real unity of the capitalist mode of production is based. What obliges the producers to participate in the construction of the world is also what separates them from it. What brings together men liberated from local and national limitations is also what keeps them apart. What pushes for greater rationality is also what nourishes the irrationality of hierarchical exploitation and repression. What creates society's abstract power also creates its concrete unfreedom.

IV

THE PROLETARIAT AS
SUBJECT AND REPRESENTATION

*The equal right of all to the goods and enjoyment of this world, the destruc-
tion of all authority, the negation of all moral restraints – these, at bottom,
are the raison d'être of the March 18th insurrection and the charter of the
fearsome organization that furnished it with an army.*

– Enquête parlementaire sur l'insurrection du 18 mars

73   THE REAL MOVEMENT that abolishes reigning conditions governed society from the moment the bourgeoisie triumphed in the economic sphere, and it did so *visibly* once that victory was translated onto the political plane. The development of the forces of production had shattered the old relations of production; every static order had crumbled to nothing. And everything that had formerly been absolute became historical.

74   IT IS BECAUSE human beings have thus been thrust into history, and into participation in the labor and the struggles which constitute history, that they find themselves obliged to view their relationships in a clear-eyed manner. The history in question has no goal aside from whatever effects it works upon itself, even though the last unconscious metaphysical vision of the historical era may view the productive progression through which history has unfolded as itself the object of that history. As for the *subject* of history, it can only be the self-production of the living: the living becoming master and possessor of its world — that is, of history — and coming to exist as *consciousness of its own activity.*

75   THE CLASS STRUGGLES of the long revolutionary period ushered in by the rise of the bourgeoisie have evolved in tandem with the "thought of history," with the dialectic — with a truly historical thinking that is not content simply to seek the meaning of what is but aspires to understand the dissolution of everything that is — and in the process to dissolve all separation.

48

76 FOR HEGEL IT was no longer a matter of interpreting the
world, but rather of interpreting the world's transformation. Inasmuch as he did *no more* than interpret that transformation, however, Hegel was merely the *philosophical*
culmination of philosophy. He sought to understand a
world that *made itself.* Such historical thought was still
part of that consciousness which comes on the scene too
late and supplies a justification after the fact. It thus transcended separation – but it did so *in thought only.* Hegel's
paradoxical posture, which subordinates the meaning of
all reality to its historical culmination, while at the same
time revealing this meaning by proclaiming *itself* to be that
culmination, arises from the simple fact that the great
thinker of the bourgeois revolutions of the seventeenth and
eighteenth centuries strove in his philosophy merely for
reconciliation with the results of those revolutions. "Even
as a philosophy of the bourgeois revolution, it does not
reflect the entire process of that revolution, but only its
concluding phase. It is thus a philosophy, not of the revolution, but of the restoration" (Karl Korsch, "Theses on
Hegel and Revolution"). Hegel performed the task of the
philosopher – "the glorification of what exists" – for the
last time, but, even for him, what existed could only be
the totality of the movement of history. Since the *external* position of thought was nevertheless maintained, this
could be masked only by identifying that thought with a
preexisting project of the Spirit – of that absolute heroic
force which has done what it willed and willed what it
has done, that force whose achievement is the present. So
philosophy, as it expires in the arms of truly historical

49

thinking, can no longer glorify its world without denying it, for even in order to express itself it must assume that the total history in which it has vested everything has come to an end, and that the only court capable of ruling on truth or falsehood has been adjourned.

77 WHEN THE PROLETARIAT demonstrates through its own actions that historical thought has not after all forgotten and lost itself, that thought's *conclusions* are negated, but at the same time the validity of its *method* is confirmed.

78 HISTORICAL THOUGHT CAN be saved only if it becomes practical thought; and the practice of the proletariat as a revolutionary class cannot be less than historical conscious-ness applied to the totality of its world. All the theoreti-cal strands of the *revolutionary* workers' movement stem from critical confrontation with Hegelian thought, and this goes for Marx as for Stirner and Bakunin.

79 THE INSEPARABILITY OF Marx's theory from the Hegelian method is itself inseparable from that theory's revolution-ary character, that is to say, from its truth. It is under this aspect that the relationship between Marx and Hegel has generally been ignored, ill understood or even denounced as the weak point of what has been fallaciously transformed into a Marxist *dogma*. Deploring the less-than-scientific predictions of the *Manifesto* of 1848 concerning the immi-nence of proletarian revolution in Germany, Bernstein per-fectly described this connection between the dialectical method and a historical *taking of sides*: "Such historical

autosuggestion, so grievously mistaken that the common-
est of political visionaries would be hard pressed to top
it, would be incomprehensible in a Marx — who by that
period had already become a serious student of the economy — were it not possible to recognize here the traces
of a lingering loyalty to Hegel's antithetical dialectics, from
which Marx, no more than Engels, had never completely
emancipated himself. In view of the general turbulence of
the times, this was all the more fatal to him."

80   THE INVERSION THAT Marx effected in order to "salvage"
the thought of the bourgeois revolutions by "transplant-
ing" it was no trivial substitution of the material development of the forces of production for the unfolding of the
Hegelian Spirit on its way to its rendezvous with itself in
time, its objectification being indistinguishable from its
alienation, and its historical wounds leaving no scars. For
history, once it becomes real, no longer has an *end*. What
Marx did was to demolish Hegel's *detached* stance with
respect to what occurs, along with the *contemplation* of a
supreme external agent of whatever kind. Theory thence-
forward had nothing to know beyond what it itself did.
By contrast, the contemplation of the movement of the
economy in the dominant thought of present-day society
is indeed a *non-inverted* legacy of the *undialectical* aspect
of the Hegelian attempt to create a circular system; this
thought is an approbatory one which no longer has the
dimension of the concept, which no longer has any need
of Hegelianism to justify it, because the movement that it
is designed to laud is a sector of the world where thought

51

no longer has any place – a sector whose mechanical development in effect dominates the world's development overall. Marx's project is the project of a conscious history whereby the quantitative realm that arises from the blind development of purely economic productive forces would be transformed into a qualitative appropriation of history. The *critique of political economy* is the first act of this *end of prehistory*: "Of all the instruments of production, the greatest productive power is the revolutionary class itself."

81   THE CLOSE AFFINITY of Marx's thinking with scientific thinking lies in its rational grasp of the forces actually at work in society. Fundamentally, though, Marx's theory lies *beyond* science, which is only preserved within it inasmuch as it is transcended by it. For Marx it is the *struggle* – and by no means the *law* – that has to be understood. "We know only a single science," says *The German Ideology*, "the science of history."

82   THE BOURGEOIS ERA, though eager to give history a scientific foundation, neglects the fact that the science available to it must certainly have been itself founded – along with the economy – on history. On the other hand, history is fundamentally dependent on economic knowledge only so long as it remains merely *economic history*. History's intervention in the economy (a global process that is after all capable of changing its own basic scientific preconditions) has in fact been overlooked by scientific observers to a degree well illustrated by the vain calculations of those socialists who believed that they could ascertain

the exact periodicity of crises. Now that continual tinkering by the State has succeeded in compensating for the tendency for crises to occur, the same type of reasoning takes this delicate balance for a permanent economic harmony. If it is to master the science of society and bring it under its governance, the project of transcending the economy and taking possession of history cannot itself be scientific in character. The revolutionary point of view, so long as it persists in espousing the notion that history in the present period can be mastered by means of scientific knowledge, has failed to rid itself of all its bourgeois traits.

83 THE UTOPIAN STRANDS in socialism, though they do have their historical roots in the critique of the existing social organization, are properly so called inasmuch as they deny history – inasmuch, that is, as they deny the struggle that exists, along with any movement of the times beyond the immutable perfection of their image of a happy society. Not, however, because they deny science. On the contrary, the utopians were completely in thrall to scientific thinking, in the form in which this had imposed itself in the preceding centuries. Their goal was the perfection of this rational system. They certainly did not look upon themselves as prophets disarmed, for they believed firmly in the social power of scientific proof – and even, in the case of Saint-Simonism, in the seizure of power by science. "However did they imagine," Sombart wonders, "that what needed to be *proved* might be won by fighting?" All the same, the utopians' scientific orientation did not extend to knowledge of the fact that social groups are liable to

53

have vested interests in a status quo, forces at their disposal equipped to maintain it and indeed forms of false consciousness designed to buttress their positions. Their idea of things thus lagged far behind the historical reality of the development of science itself, which was by this time largely governed by the *social demand* arising from factors, such as those mentioned above, which determined not only what was considered scientifically acceptable but also just what might become an object of scientific research. The utopian socialists remained prisoners to the *scientific manner of expounding the truth*, and they viewed this truth in accordance with its pure abstract image – the form in which it had established itself at a much earlier moment in social development. As Sorel noted, the utopians took *astronomy* as their model for the discovery and demonstration of the laws of society: their conception of harmony, so hostile to history, was the product, logically enough, of an attempted application to society of the science least dependent on history. This conception was introduced and promoted with an experimental ingenuousness worthy of Newtonism, and the smiling future continually evoked by the utopians played "a role in their social science analogous to that played by inertia in rational mechanics" (*Matériaux pour une théorie du prolétariat*).

84 THE SCIENTIFIC-DETERMINIST side of Marx's thought was indeed what made it vulnerable to "ideologization"; the breach was opened in Marx's own lifetime, and greatly widened in his theoretical legacy to the workers' movement. The advent of the subject of history was conse-

quently set back even further, as economics, the historical science par excellence, was depended on more and more as guarantor of the necessity of its own future negation. In this way *revolutionary practice* — the only true agent of this negation — tended to be thrust out of theory's field of vision altogether. It became important patiently to study economic development, and once more to accept, with Hegelian tranquillity, the suffering it imposed — that suffering whose outcome was still a "graveyard of good intentions." All of a sudden it was discovered that, according to the "science of revolutions," *consciousness now always came on the scene too soon*, and needed to be taught. "History has proved us, and all who thought like us, wrong," Engels would write in 1895. "It has made it clear that the state of economic development on the Continent at that time was not, by a long way, ripe...." Throughout his life Marx upheld his theory's unitary standpoint, yet in the *exposition* of that theory he was drawn onto the ground of the dominant forms of thought, in that he undertook critiques of particular disciplines, and notably that of the fundamental science of bourgeois society, political economy. It was in this mutilated form, later taken as definitive, that Marx's theory became "Marxism."

85 THE WEAKNESS OF Marx's theory is naturally part and parcel of the weakness of the revolutionary struggle of the proletariat of his time. The working class failed to inaugurate permanent revolution in 1848, and the Commune went down in isolation. Revolutionary theory was thus still unable to come into full possession of its own existence.

That Marx should have been reduced to defending and honing that theory in the detachment of scholarly work in the British Museum can only have had a debilitating effect on the theory itself. What is certain is that the scientific conclusions that Marx drew about the future development of the working class — along with the organizational practice founded on them — would later become obstacles to proletarian consciousness.

86 ALL THE THEORETICAL shortcomings of a *scientific* defense of proletarian revolution, be they in the content or in the form of the exposition, come down in the end to the identification of the proletariat with the bourgeoisie *with respect to the revolutionary seizure of power.*

87 AS EARLY AS the *Manifesto*, the urge to demonstrate the scientific legitimacy of proletarian power by citing a sequence of precedents only served to muddy Marx's historical thinking. This approach led him to defend a linear model of the development of modes of production according to which, at each stage, class struggles would end "either in a revolutionary reconstitution of society at large, or in the common ruin of the contending classes." The plain facts of history, however, are that, just as the "Asiatic mode of production" (as Marx himself observed in another connection) preserved its stasis in spite of class conflict, so too no *jacquerie* of serfs ever overthrew the barons and no slave revolt in the ancient world ever ended the rule of freemen. The first thing the linear model loses sight of is the fact that *the bourgeoisie is the only revolutionary class that*

has ever been victorious; the only class, also, for which the development of the economy was the cause and consequence of its capture of society. The same simplified view led Marx to neglect the economic role of the State in the management of a class society. If the rising bourgeoisie appears to have liberated the economy from the State, this is true only to the extent that the State was formerly the instrument of class oppression in a *static economy*. The bourgeoisie developed its autonomous economic power during the medieval period when the State had been weakened, when feudalism was breaking up a stable equilibrium between powers. The modern State, on the other hand, which first supported the developing bourgeoisie thanks to the mercantile system, and then went on, in the time of "laisser faire, laisser passer," to become the bourgeoisie's *own State*, was eventually to emerge as wielder of a power central to the planned management of the *economic process*. Marx was already able, under the rubric of Bonapartism, accurately to depict a foreshadowing of modern State bureaucracy in that fusion of capital and State which established "capital's national power over labor and a public authority designed to maintain social servitude"; the bourgeoisie thus renounced any historical existence beyond its own reduction to the economic history of *things*, and permitted itself to be "condemned along with the other classes to a like political nullity." Already discernible in outline here are the sociopolitical bases of the modern spectacle, which in a negative way defines the proletariat as *the only pretender to historical existence*.

88   THE ONLY TWO classes that really correspond to Marx's theory, the two pure classes that the whole thrust of *Capital*'s analysis tends to bring to the fore, are the bourgeoisie and the proletariat. These are also the only two revolutionary classes in history – but they are revolutionary under different conditions. The bourgeois revolution is a fait accompli. The proletarian revolution is a project, formulated on the basis of the earlier revolution but differing qualitatively from it. To neglect the originality of the bourgeoisie's historical role serves only to conceal the concrete originality of the proletarian project, which can get nowhere unless it advances under its own banner and comes to grips with the "prodigiousness of its own aims." The bourgeoisie came to power because it was the class of the developing economy. The proletariat will never come to embody power unless it becomes the *class of consciousness*. The growth of the forces of production cannot in itself guarantee this accession to power – not even indirectly, via the increase in dispossession that this growth entails. Nor can any Jacobin-style seizure of the State be a means to that end. The proletariat cannot make use of any *ideology* designed to pass partial goals off as general ones, because it cannot maintain any partial reality that is truly its own.

89   IT IS TRUE that during a certain period of his participation in the struggle of the proletariat Marx overrated the value of scientific prediction – indeed he went so far in this direction that he provided the illusions of economism with an intellectual justification; however, he clearly never fell prey himself to such illusions. In a well-known letter

of 7 December 1867, accompanying an article criticizing *Capital* which he himself had written, and which Engels was supposed to publish as if it were that of an opponent, Marx clearly indicated the limits of his scientific stance: "The author's *subjective* tendency (imposed on him, perhaps, by his political position and his past) — that is to say, the way in which he himself pictures, and portrays for others, the ultimate outcome of the present movement, the present social process — has nothing whatsoever to do with his real analysis." By thus censuring the "tendentious conclusions" of his own objective analysis, and by interpolating an ironic "perhaps" apropos of the unscientific choices supposedly "imposed" on him, Marx in effect reveals the methodological key to tackling the two aspects of the matter.

90 THE FUSION OF knowledge and action must be effected within the historical struggle itself, in such a way that each of these poles depends for its validation on the other. What constitutes the proletarian class as a subject is its organizing of revolutionary struggles and its organizing of society at the *moment of revolution*: this is the point at which the *practical conditions of consciousness* must be assembled and the theory of praxis verified by virtue of its transformation into theory-in-practice. This pivotal issue of organization, however, received but the scantest attention from revolutionary theory during the founding period of the workers' movement — the very period when that theory still possessed the unitary character which it had inherited from historical thought (and which it had rightly vowed

to develop into a unitary historical *practice*). As it turned out, organization became the locus of revolutionary theory's *inconsistency*, allowing the tenets of that theory to be *imposed* by statist and hierarchical methods borrowed from the bourgeois revolution. The forms of organization developed subsequently by the workers' movement on the basis of this dereliction of theory have tended in turn to bar the construction of a unitary theory, to break theory up instead into a variety of specialized and fragmentary types of knowledge. Thus ideologically alienated, theory cannot even recognize the practical verification of the unitary historical thought that it has betrayed whenever that verification emerges in spontaneous workers' struggles; on the contrary, all it can do is help to repress it and destroy all memory of it. Yet such historical forms, thrown up by the struggle, are the very practical medium that theory needs in order to be true. They are in fact a requirement of theory, but one that has not been given theoretical expression. The soviets, for example, were not a theoretical discovery; and, to go back even farther, the highest *theoretical* truth attained by the International Workingmen's Association was its own existence *in practice*.

91 EARLY SUCCESSES IN the First International's struggle enabled it to free itself from the confused influences that the dominant ideology continued for a time to exercise upon it from within. But the defeat and repression that it soon confronted brought to the surface a conflict between two conceptions of the proletarian revolution, each of which had an *authoritarian* dimension spelling the abandonment

of the conscious self-emancipation of the working class. The rift between Marxists and Bakuninists, which eventually became an irreconcilable one, had a dual aspect in that it bore both upon the question of power in a future revolutionary society and upon the current organization of the movement; and both the opposing factions reversed their own position in moving from one of these issues to the other. Bakunin denounced as an illusion the idea that classes could be abolished by means of an authoritarian use of State power, warning that this course would lead to the reconstruction of a bureaucratic ruling class and to the dictatorship of the most knowledgeable (or of those reputed to be the most knowledgeable). Marx, who held that the combined maturation, of economic contradictions on the one hand, and of the democratic education of the. workers on the other hand, would reduce the proletarian State's role to the short phase needed to give the stamp of legality to new social relations brought into being by objective factors, charged Bakunin and his supporters with the authoritarianism of a conspiratorial elite that had deliberately placed itself above the International with the harebrained intention of imposing on society an irresponsible dictatorship of the most revolutionary (or of those self-designated as such). Bakunin unquestionably recruited followers on just such a basis: "in the midst of the popular tempest, we must be the invisible pilots guiding the Revolution, not by any kind of overt power but by the collective dictatorship of all our allies, a dictatorship without badges, without official titles, without any official status, and therefore all the more powerful, as it does not carry the trappings of power." This was clearly a clash between two *ideologies* of workers' revolution; each embodied a partially correct critique, but each, having lost the unity of historical thought, aspired to set itself up as an ideological *authority*. Powerful organizations, among them the German Social Democracy and the Iberian Anarchist Federation, would subsequently faithfully serve one or the other of these ideologies; in every case the result produced was greatly different from the one sought.

92 THE FACT THAT the anarchists regard the goal of the proletarian revolution as *immediately present* is at once the great strength and the great weakness of the real anarchist struggle (I refer to the struggle of *collectivist* anarchism; the claims of anarchism in its individualist variants are laughable). Collectivist anarchism retains only the *terminal point* of the historical thought of modern class struggles, and its unconditional demand that this point be attained instantly is echoed in its systematic contempt for method. Its critique of the *political struggle* consequently remains an abstract one, while its commitment to the economic struggle is framed only in terms of the mirage of a definitive solution to be achieved at one stroke, on the economic battleground itself, on the day of the general strike or insurrection. The anarchist agenda is the *fulfillment of an ideal*. Anarchism is the *still ideological* negation of the State and of classes, that is to say, of the very social preconditions of any separated ideology. It is an *ideology of pure freedom* which makes everything equal and eschews any suggestion of historical evil. This position, which fuses

all partial demands into a single demand, has given anarchism the great merit of representing the refusal of existing
conditions from the standpoint of the whole of life, not
merely from the standpoint of some particular critical specialization. On the other hand, the fact that this fusion of
demands is envisaged in the absolute, at the whim of the
individual, and in advance of any actualization, has doomed
anarchism to an incoherence that is only too easy to dis-
cern: the doctrine requires no more than the reiteration,
and the reintroduction into each particular struggle, of the
same simple and all-encompassing idea – the same end-
point that anarchism has identified from the first as the
movement's sole and entire goal. Thus Bakunin, on quit-
ting the Jura Federation in 1873, found it easy to write that
"During the last nine years more than enough ideas for the
salvation of the world have been developed in the International (if the world can be saved by ideas) and I defy anyone to come up with a new one. This is the time not for
ideas but for action, for deeds." No doubt this attitude preserves the commitment of the truly historical thought of
the proletariat to the notion that ideas must become practical, but it leaves the ground of history by assuming that the
adequate forms of this transition to practice have already
been discovered and are no longer subject to variation.

93 THE ANARCHISTS, whose ideological fervor clearly distinguished them from the rest of the workers' movement,
extended this specialization of tasks into their own ranks,
so offering a hospitable field of action, within any anarchist organization, to the propagandists and defenders of

anarchist ideology; and the mediocrity of these specialists was only reinforced by the fact that their intellectual activity was generally confined to the repetition of a clutch of unchanging truths. An ideological respect for unanimity in the taking of decisions tended to favor the uncontrolled exercise of power, within the organization itself, by "specialists of freedom"; and revolutionary anarchism expects a comparable unanimity, obtained by comparable means, from the people once they are liberated. Furthermore, the refusal to distinguish between the opposed situations of a minority grouped in the ongoing struggle and a new society of free individuals has led time and again to the permanent isolation of anarchists when the time for common decisions arrives – one need only think of the countless anarchist insurrections in Spain that have been contained and crushed at a local level.

94   THE ILLUSION MORE OR LESS explicitly upheld in all genuine anarchism is that of the permanent imminence of a revolution which, because it will be made instantaneously, is bound to validate both anarchist ideology and the form of practical organization that flows from it. In 1936 anarchism really did lead a social revolution, setting up the most advanced model of proletarian power ever realized. Even here, though, it is pertinent to recall, for one thing, that the general insurrection was dictated by an army pronunciamento. Furthermore, inasmuch as the revolution was not completed in its earliest days – Franco, enjoying strong foreign backing at a time when the rest of the international proletarian movement had already been defeated,

held power in half the country, while bourgeois forces and other workers' parties of statist bent still existed in the Republican camp – the organized anarchist movement proved incapable of broadening the revolution's semi-victories, or even of safeguarding them. The movement's leaders became government ministers – hostages to a bourgeois state that was dismantling the revolution even as it proceeded to lose the civil war.

95 THE "ORTHODOX MARXISM" of the Second International was the scientific ideology of the socialist revolution, an ideology which asserted that its whole truth resided in objective economic processes, and in the gradual recognition of their necessity by a working class educated by the organization. This ideology exhumed utopian socialism's faith in pedagogics, eking this out with a *contemplative* evocation of the course of history. So out of touch was this attitude with the Hegelian dimension of a total history, however, that it lost even the static image of the totality present in the utopians' (and signally in Fourier's) critique. A scientific orientation of this variety, hardly capable of doing anything more than rehash symmetrical ethical alternatives, informed Hilferding's insipid observation in *Das Finanzkapital* that recognizing the necessity of socialism "gives no clue as to what practical attitude should be adopted. For it is one thing to recognize a necessity, and quite another to place oneself in the service of that necessity." Those who chose not to understand that for Marx, and for the revolutionary proletariat, a unitary historical thought was itself *nothing more and nothing less than the*

65

practical attitude to be adopted could only fall victim to the practice which that choice immediately entailed.

96   THE IDEOLOGY OF the social-democratic organization placed that organization in the hands of *teachers* who were supposed to educate the working class, and the organizational form adopted corresponded perfectly to the sort of passive learning that this implied. The participation of the socialists of the Second International in the political and economic struggles was concrete enough, but it was profoundly *uncritical*. Theirs was a manifestly *reformist* practice carried on in the name of an *illusory revolution*. It was inevitable that this ideology of revolution should founder on the very success of those who proclaimed it. The setting apart of parliamentary representatives and journalists within the movement encouraged people who had in any case been recruited from the bourgeois intelligentsia to pursue a bourgeois style of life, while the trade-union bureaucracy turned even those drawn in through industrial struggle, and of working-class background, into mere brokers of labor — traders in labor-power as a commodity to be bought and sold like any other. For the activity of all these people to have retained any revolutionary aspect whatsoever, capitalism would have had to find itself conveniently unable to put up with a reformism on the economic plane that it was perfectly able to tolerate on the political, in the shape of the social democrats' legalistic agitation. The "science" of the social democrats vouched for the inevitability of such a paradoxical occurrence; history, however, gave the lie to it at every turn.

97 THIS WAS A CONTRADICTION that Bernstein, being the
social democrat farthest removed from political ideology, and the one who most unabashedly embraced the
methodology of bourgeois science, was honest enough to
draw attention to; the reformism of the English workers'
movement, which did without revolutionary ideology
altogether, also attested to it; but only historical development itself could demonstrate it beyond all possibility
of doubt. Though prey to all kinds of illusions in other
areas, Bernstein had rejected the notion that a crisis of
capitalism must miraculously occur, thus forcing the hand
of the socialists, who declined to assume any revolutionary mantle in the absence of such a legitimating event.
The profound social upheaval set in train by the First
World War, though it raised consciousness on a wide
scale, proved twice over that the social-democratic hier-
archy had failed to educate the German workers in a revolutionary way, that it had failed, in short, to *turn them
into theoreticians*: the first time was when the overwhelm-
ing majority of the party lent its support to the imperialist war; the second time was when, in defeat, the party
crushed the Spartacist revolutionaries. The sometime
worker Ebert still believed in sin — declaring that he
hated revolution "like sin." He also proved himself to be
a fine herald of that *image of socialism* which was soon to
emerge as the mortal enemy of the proletariat of Russia
and elsewhere, by precisely articulating the agenda of this
new form of alienation: "Socialism," said Ebert, "means
working hard."

98 AS A MARXIST THINKER, Lenin was simply a faithful and consistent Kautskyist who applied the *revolutionary ideology* of "orthodox Marxism" to the conditions existing in Russia, conditions that did not permit of the sort of reformist practice pursued in parallel fashion by the Second International. The task of directing the proletariat from without, by means of a disciplined clandestine party under the control of intellectuals who had become "professional revolutionaries," gave rise to a genuine *profession* – and one disinclined to make compacts with any professional strata of capitalist society (even had such an overture – presupposing the attainment of an advanced stage of bourgeois development – been within the power of the czarist political regime to make). In consequence the speciality of the profession in question became that of *total social management.*

99 WITH THE ADVENT OF the war, and the collapse of international social democracy in face of it, the authoritarian ideological radicalism of the Bolsheviks was able to cast its net across the globe. The bloody end of the workers' movement's democratic illusions made a Russia of the whole world, and Bolshevism, reigning over the first revolutionary rift opened up by this period of crisis, proposed its hierarchical and ideological model to the proletariat of all countries as the way to "talk Russian" to the ruling class. Lenin never reproached the Second International's Marxism for being a revolutionary *ideology* – but only for having ceased to be such an ideology.

100   THIS SAME HISTORICAL MOMENT, when Bolshevism triumphed *for itself* in Russia and social democracy fought
victoriously *for the old world*, also marks the definitive
inauguration of an order of things that lies at the core of
the modern spectacle's rule: this was the moment when
an *image of the working class* arose in radical opposition to
the working class itself.

101   "IN ALL EARLIER REVOLUTIONS," wrote Rosa Luxem-
burg in *Die Rote Fahne* for 21 December 1918, "the opponents confronted one another face to face: class against
class, program against program. In the present revolution,
the troops that protect the old order, instead of interven-
ing in the name of the ruling classes, intervene under the
banner of a 'social-democratic party.' If the central question of the revolution were posed openly and honestly –
in the form 'Capitalism or socialism?' – then no doubt or
hesitation would be possible today among the broad proletarian masses." Thus, a few days before its destruction,
the radical current within the German proletariat uncov-
ered the secret of the new conditions brought into being
by the whole process which had gone before (and to which
the *image* of the working class had largely contributed):
the spectacular organization of the ruling order's defense,
and a social reign of appearances under which no "central question" could any longer be "openly and honestly"
posed. By this time the revolutionary image of the proletariat had become both the main element in, and the chief
result of, a general falsification of society.

102 THE ORGANIZATION OF the proletariat according to the
Bolshevik model stemmed from the backwardness of Russia and from the abdication from the revolutionary struggle of the workers' movement in the advanced countries.
Russian backwardness also embodied all the conditions
needed to carry this form of organization in the direction
of the counterrevolutionary reversal that it had unconsciously contained from its beginnings; and the repeated
balking of the mass of the European workers' movement
at the *Hic Rhodus, hic salta* of the 1918–1920 period – a
balking that included the violent annihilation of its own
radical minority – further facilitated the complete unfolding of a process whose end result could fraudulently present itself to the world as the only possible proletarian
solution. The Bolshevik party justified itself in terms of
the necessity of a State monopoly over the representation
and defense of the power of the workers, and its success in
this quest turned the party into what it truly was, namely
the party of the *owners of the proletariat*, which essentially
dislodged all earlier forms of ownership.

103 FOR TWENTY YEARS the various tendencies of Russian
social democracy had engaged in an unresolved debate over
which conditions were most propitious for the overthrow
of czarism: the weakness of the bourgeoisie, the weight
in the balance of the peasant majority, the decisive role
to be played by a centralized and militant proletariat, and
so on. When practice finally provided the solution, however, it did so thanks to a factor that had figured in none
of these hypotheses, namely the revolutionary bureaucracy

which placed itself at the head of the proletariat, seized the State and proceeded to impose a new form of class rule on society. A strictly bourgeois revolution was impossible; talk of a "democratic dictatorship of workers and peasants" had no real meaning; and, as for the proletarian power of the soviets, it could not be maintained at once against the class of small landholding peasants, against a national and international White reaction, and against its own external-ized and alienated representation in the shape of a workers' party of absolute masters of the State, of the economy, of the means of expression and (before long) of thought. Trotsky and Parvus's theory of permanent revolution – which Lenin in effect espoused in April 1917 – was the only theory that held true for countries that were back-ward from the point of view of the social development of the bourgeoisie, but even here it only applied once the unknown quantity of the bureaucracy's class power had come into play. In the many clashes within the Bolshevik leadership, Lenin was the most consistent defender of the concentration of dictatorial powers in the hands of this supreme ideological representation. He invariably had the advantage over his opponents because he championed solu-tions that flowed logically from the earlier choices made by the minority that now exercised absolute power: a democ-racy refused to peasants *on the State level* should be by the same token refused to workers, and hence also to Com-munist union leaders, to party members in general, and even, in the end, to the highest ranks of the party's hier-archy. At the Tenth Congress, as the Kronstadt soviet was being put down by force of arms and deluged in slander,

71

Lenin passed a judgment on the leftist bureaucrats of the "Workers' Opposition," the logic of which Stalin would later extend into a perfect division of the world: "Here with us – or out there with a gun in your hand – but not as an opposition. We have had enough of opposition."

104   FINDING ITSELF the sole owner of a *state capitalism*, the bureaucracy at first secured its power internally by entering, after Kronstadt, and under the "New Economic Policy," into a temporary alliance with the peasantry; externally, in parallel fashion, it defended its power by using the regimented workers of the bureaucratic parties of the Third International to back up Russian diplomacy, to sabotage revolutionary movements and to support bourgeois governments on whose support in the international sphere it was counting (the Kuomintang in the China of 1925–1927, Popular Fronts in Spain and France, etc.). In pursuit of its self-realization, however, bureaucratic society then proceeded, by means of terror exercised against the peasantry, to effect history's most brutal primitive accumulation of capital ever. The industrialization of the Stalin era reveals the *bureaucracy's true nature*: the prolonging of the reign of the economy and the salvaging of all essential aspects of market society, not least the institution of labor-as-commodity. The economy in its independence thus showed itself so thoroughly able to dominate society as to recreate for its own purposes that class domination which is essential to its operation. It proved, in other words, that the bourgeoisie had created a power so autonomous that, so long as it endured, it could even do without a bourgeoi-

sie. The totalitarian bureaucracy was not, in Bruno Rizzi's sense, "the last property-owning class in history," for it was merely a *substitute ruling class* for the market economy. A tottering capitalist property system was replaced by an inferior version of itself – simplified, less diversified and *concentrated* as the collective property of the bureaucratic class. This underdeveloped type of ruling class was likewise a reflection of economic underdevelopment, and it had no agenda beyond correcting this backwardness in particular parts of the world. The hierarchical, statist framework for this cheap remake of the capitalist ruling class was supplied by the party of the workers, organized on the bourgeois model of *separation*. As Anton Ciliga noted from the depths of one of Stalin's prisons, "Technical questions of organization turned out to be social questions" (*Lenin and Revolution*).

105   AS THE *coherence of the separate*, the revolutionary ideology of which Leninism was the highest voluntaristic expression governed the management of a reality that was resistant to it; with Stalinism, this ideology rediscovered its own incoherent essence. Ideology was no longer a weapon, but an end in itself. But a lie that can no longer be challenged becomes a form of madness. Eventually both reality and the goal sought dissolved in a totalitarian ideology proclaiming that whatever it said was *all there was*. This was a local primitivism of the spectacle that has nonetheless played an essential part in the spectacle's worldwide development. The ideology that took on material form in this context did not transform the world economically, as

73

capitalism in its affluent stage has done; it succeeded only in using police methods to transform *perception*.

106　THE IDEOLOGICAL-TOTALITARIAN class in power is the power of a world turned on its head: the stronger the class, the more forcefully it proclaims that it does not exist, and its strength serves first and foremost to assert its nonexistence. This is as far as its modesty goes, however, for its official nonexistence is supposed to coincide with the *ne plus ultra* of historical development, which is indeed owed to its infallible leadership. Though everywhere in evidence, the bureaucracy is obliged to be a class imperceptible to consciousness, thus making the whole of social life unfathomable and insane. The social organization of the absolute lie reposes on this fundamental contradiction.

107　STALINISM WAS a reign of terror *within* the bureaucratic class. The terror on which the bureaucracy's power was founded was bound to strike the class itself, because this class had no legal basis, no juridical status as a property-owning class that could be extended to each of its members individually. Its real proprietorship was masked, because it had become an owner only by means of false consciousness. False consciousness can maintain absolute power only through absolute terror, where all real motives soon vanish. Members of the ruling bureaucratic class have the right of ownership over society only collectively, as participants in a basic lie: they have to play the part of the proletariat governing a socialist society; they are actors faithful to the

74

text of ideological betrayal. Yet their effective participation in this counterfeit being has to be perceived as real. No bureaucrat can individually assert his right to power, because to prove himself a socialist proletarian he would have to present himself as the opposite of a bureaucrat, while to prove himself a bureaucrat is impossible because the official truth of the bureaucracy is that the bureaucracy does not exist. Thus each bureaucrat is completely dependent on a central guarantee from ideology, which acknowledges the collective participation in "socialist power" of *all such bureaucrats as it does not liquidate*. As a group the bureaucrats may be said to make all the decisions, but the cohesiveness of their class can only be ensured by the concentration of their terroristic power in one person. In this person reposes the only practical truth of the lie *in power*: the power to lay down an unchallengeable boundary that is ever subject to revision. Stalin thus had the power to decide without appeal exactly who was a bureaucrat, and hence an owner; his word alone distinguished "proletarians" in power from "traitors in the pay of the Mikado and Wall Street." The atomized bureaucrat could find the shared essence of his juridical status only in the *person* of Stalin — that lord and master of the world who takes himself in this way to be the absolute person and for whom there exists no higher type of spirit: "The lord of the world becomes really conscious of what he is — viz., the universal might of actuality — by that power of destruction which he exercises against the contrasted selfhood of his subjects." He is at once the power that defines the field of domination and the power that devastates that field.

75

108 BY THE TIME IDEOLOGY, become absolute because it pos-
sesses absolute power, has been transformed from a fragmentary knowledge into a totalitarian lie, truly historical
thinking has for its part been so utterly annihilated that history itself, even at the level of the most empirical knowledge, can no longer exist. Totalitarian bureaucratic society
lives in a perpetual present in which everything that has
happened earlier exists for it solely as a space accessible
to its police. A project already formulated by Napoleon,
that of "monarchically directing the energy of memories,"
has thus been made concrete in a permanent manipula-
tion of the past, and this not just in respect of the past's
meaning, but even in respect of the facts themselves. The
price paid for this emancipation from all historical reality, though, is the loss of the rational orientation indispensable to capitalism as a *historical* social system. We know
how much the scientific application of an ideology gone
mad has cost Russia – one need only think of the Lysenko
fiasco. The internal contradictions besetting totalitarian
bureaucracy in its administration of an industrialized society – its simultaneous need for rationality and refusal
of it – also constitutes one of its chief shortcomings as
compared with normal capitalist development. Just as the
bureaucracy cannot resolve the question of agriculture as
capitalism does, so too it turns out eventually to be inferior to capitalism in industrial production, which it seeks
to plan in an authoritarian manner on the twin bases of
a complete lack of realism and an adherence to an all-
embracing lie.

109   BETWEEN THE TWO world wars the revolutionary workers'
movement was destroyed by the action, on the one hand,
of the Stalinist bureaucracy and, on the other, of fascist
totalitarianism, the latter having borrowed its organizational form from the totalitarian party as first tried out in
Russia. Fascism was an attempt of the bourgeois economy
to defend itself, *in extremis*, from the dual threat of crisis
and proletarian subversion; it was a *state of siege* in capitalist society, a way for that society to survive through the
administration of an emergency dose of rationalization in
the form of massive State intervention in its management.
Such rationalization, however, inevitably bore the stamp
of the immensely irrational nature of the means whereby
it was imposed. Even though fascism came to the aid of
the chief icons (the family, private property, the moral
order, the nation) of a bourgeois order that was by now
conservative, and effectively mobilized both the petty bourgeoisie and unemployed workers panic-stricken because of
the crisis or disillusioned by the impotence of revolutionary socialism, it was not itself fundamentally ideological
in character. Fascism presented itself for what it was – a
violent resurrection of *myth* calling for participation in a
community defined by archaic pseudo-values: race, blood,
leader. Fascism is a cult of the archaic completely fitted
out by modern technology. Its degenerate ersatz of myth
has been revived in the spectacular context of the most
modern means of conditioning and illusion. It is thus one
factor in the formation of the modern spectacle, as well
as being, thanks to its part in the destruction of the old
workers' movement, one of the founding forces of present-

77

day society. But inasmuch as fascism happens also to be the *costliest* method of maintaining the capitalist order, it was normal enough that it should be dislodged by more rational and stronger forms of this order – that it should leave the front of the stage to the lead players, namely the capitalist States.

110 WHEN THE RUSSIAN BUREAUCRACY at last successfully disencumbered itself of relics of bourgeois property standing in the way of its hegemony over the economy, once it had developed this economy in accordance with its own purposes, and once it had achieved recognition from without as a great power among others, it sought to enjoy its own world in tranquillity, and to remove the arbitrariness to which it was still itself subjected; it therefore proceeded to denounce the Stalinism of its beginnings. Such a denunciation was bound, however, to remain Stalinist, arbitrary, unexplained and subject to continual adjustment, for the simple reason that *the ideological falsehood that had attended the bureaucracy's birth could never be exposed.* The bureaucracy cannot liberalize itself either culturally or politically because its existence as a class depends on its monopoly of an ideology – which, for all its cumbersomeness, is its sole title to ownership. Admittedly this ideology has lost the passion that informed its original self-affirmation, yet even the pithless triviality which is all that is left retains the oppressive role of prohibiting the least suggestion of competition and holding the entirety of thought captive. The bureaucracy is thus helplessly tied to an ideology no longer believed by anyone. What inspired

terror now inspires derision, but even this derision would disappear were it not for the fact that the terror it mocks still lurks in the wings. So it is that at the very moment when the bureaucracy attempts to demonstrate its superiority on capitalism's own ground, it is exposed as capitalism's *poor cousin*. Just as its actual history is at odds with its judicial status, and its crudely maintained ignorance in contradiction with its scientific pretensions, so its wish to vie with the bourgeoisie in the production of an abundance of commodities is stymied by the fact that an abundance of this kind contains *its own implicit ideology*, and is generally accompanied by the freedom to choose from an unlimited range of spectacular false alternatives – a pseudo-freedom, yes, but one which, for all that, is incompatible with the bureaucracy's ideology.

111 AT THE PRESENT STAGE in the bureaucracy's development, its ideological title to ownership is already collapsing internationally: a power set up on the national level as a basically internationalist model must now renounce any claim to maintaining its false cohesion irrespective of national frontiers. The unequal economic development experienced by those competing bureaucracies that have succeeded in owning "socialism" in more than one country has led only to a public and all-out confrontation between the Russian lie and the Chinese lie. Henceforward each bureaucracy in power, and likewise each of those totalitarian parties aspiring to a power that has outlived the Stalinist period within one national working class or another, will have to find its own way. Considered in con-

79

junction with the expressions of internal negation which first became visible to the outside world when the workers of East Berlin revolted against the bureaucrats and demanded a "government of metalworkers," and which have since even extended to the setting up of workers' councils in Hungary, this crumbling of the worldwide alliance founded on bureaucratic mystification is in the last analysis the most unfavorable portent for the future development of capitalist society. For the bourgeoisie is now in danger of losing an adversary that has objectively supported it by investing all opposition to its order with a purely illusory unity. A rift in the pseudo-revolutionary component of the established division of spectacular labor can only herald the end of that system itself. This spectacular aspect of the dissolution of the workers' movement is thus itself headed for dissolution.

112 THE MIRAGE OF LENINISM today has no basis today outside the various Trotskyist tendencies, where the conflation of the proletarian project with a hierarchical organization grounded in ideology has stolidly survived all the evidence of that conflation's real consequences. The gap between Trotskyism and a revolutionary critique of present-day society is in effect coextensive with the respectful distance that the Trotskyists maintain toward positions that were already mistaken when they played themselves out in a real struggle. Until 1927 Trotsky remained fundamentally loyal to the high bureaucracy, though he sought to gain control of this bureaucracy and cause it to resume a properly Bolshevik foreign policy. (It is well known that at this time

he went so far, in order to help conceal Lenin's famous "Testament," as to disavow slanderously his supporter Max Eastman, who had made it public.) Trotsky was doomed by his basic perspective; the fact was that as soon as the bureaucratic class knew itself, on the basis of the results of its action, to be a counterrevolutionary class on the domestic front, it was bound to opt for a counterrevolutionary role on the world stage, albeit one assumed in the name of revolution – in short, to act abroad *just as it did at home.* Trotsky's subsequent struggle to set up a Fourth International enshrined the same inconsistency. Having once, during the second Russian revolution, become an unconditional partisan of the Bolshevik form of organization, Trotsky simply refused, for the rest of his life, to see that the bureaucracy's power was the power of a separate class. When Lukács, in 1923, pointed to this same organizational form as the long-sought mediation between theory and practice thanks to which proletarians, instead of being mere "spectators" of events that occur in their own organization, consciously choose and experience those events, what he was describing as actual virtues of the Bolshevik party were in fact everything that the Party *was not.* The depth of his theoretical work notwithstanding, Lukács was an ideologist speaking for a power that was in the crudest way external to the proletarian movement, believing and giving his audience to believe that he himself, his entire personal being, partook of this power as though it were truly *his own.* While subsequent events were to demonstrate exactly how the power in question repudiated and eliminated its servants, Lukács, with his endless self-repudiations, revealed with caricatural clarity precisely what he had identified with, namely, the opposite of himself, and the opposite of everything for which he had argued in *History and Class Consciousness*. No one better than Lukács illustrates the validity of a fundamental rule for assessing all the intellectuals of this century: what they *respect* is a precise gauge of their own *contemptible* reality. It certainly cannot be said that Lenin encouraged illusions of this kind concerning his activities, for it was Lenin who acknowledged that "a political party cannot examine its members to see whether contradictions exist between their philosophy and the party program." The real subject of Lukács's purely imaginary — and inopportune — portrait was a party that was indeed coherent with respect to one precise and partial task only — to wit, the seizure of State power.

113　THE NEO-LENINIST mirage entertained by present-day Trotskyism is contradicted at every moment by the reality of modern capitalist society, whether of the bourgeois or the bureaucratic type. It is therefore not surprising that it gets its best reception in the formally independent "underdeveloped" countries, where a variety of fraudulent versions of state and bureaucratic socialism are consciously passed off by local ruling classes as, quite simply, *the* ideology of economic development. The hybrid nature of such classes is more or less directly associated with their position on the bourgeois-bureaucratic spectrum. Their international maneuvering between these two poles of existing capitalist power, along with ideological compro-

mises (notably with Islam) corresponding to their heter-
ogeneous social bases, together serve to strip these last
retreads of ideological socialism of all credibility except
for that of their police. One type of bureaucracy has established itself by providing a common framework for nation-
alist struggle and peasant agrarian revolt; in such cases, as
in China, the Stalinist model of industrialization tends to
be applied in societies even less advanced than the Russia
of 1917. A bureaucracy capable of industrializing a nation
may also arise out of the petty bourgeoisie, with power
being seized by army officers, as happened for instance in
Egypt. In other places, among them Algeria following its
war of independence, a bureaucracy that has established
itself as a para-State authority in the course of a struggle
seeks stability through compromise, and fuses with a weak
national bourgeoisie. Lastly, in those former colonies of
black Africa that have maintained overt ties to Western
bourgeoisies, whether European or American, a local bourgeoisie is constituted – generally reposing on the power
of traditional tribal chiefs – *through possession of the State*:
in such countries, where foreign imperialism is still the
true master of the economy, a stage is reached at which
the compradors' compensation for the sale of local products is ownership of a local State that is independent of
the masses though not of the imperialist power. The result
is an artificial bourgeoisie that is incapable of accumulating capital and merely *squanders* its revenue – as much
the portion of surplus value it extracts from local labor as
the foreign subsidies it receives from protector States or
monopolies. The manifest incapacity of such a bourgeoi-

sie to fulfill normal bourgeois economic functions leads to its soon being confronted by a subversive opposition, structured on the bureaucratic model and more or less well adapted to local conditions, that is eager to usurp what the bourgeoisie has inherited. But the successful realization by any bureaucracy of its fundamental project of industrialization itself necessarily embodies the prospect of its historical failure, for as it accumulates capital it also accumulates the proletariat, so creating its own negation in countries where that negation did not yet exist.

114   IN THE COURSE OF the complex and terrible evolution that has brought the era of class struggle under a new set of conditions, the proletariat of the industrialized countries has lost the ability to assert its own independence. It has also, in the last reckoning, lost its *illusions*. But it has not lost its being. The proletariat has not been eliminated, and indeed it remains irreducibly present, under the intensified alienation of modern capitalism, in the shape of the vast mass of workers who have lost all power over the use of their own lives and who, *once they realize this*, must necessarily redefine themselves as the proletariat — as negation at work in the bosom of today's society. This class is objectively reinforced by the peasantry's gradual disappearance, as also by the extension of the logic of the factory system to a broad sector of labor in the "services" and the intellectual professions. *Subjectively*, though, this is a proletariat still very far removed from any practical class consciousness, and this goes not only for white-collar workers but also for wage workers who as yet know nothing

84

but the impotence and mystifications of the old politics. But when the proletariat discovers that its own external- ized power conspires in the continual reinforcement of capitalist society, no longer merely thanks to the aliena- tion of its labor, but also thanks to the form taken on by unions, parties and institutions of State power that it had established in pursuit of its own self-emancipation, then it must also discover through concrete historical experi- ence that it is indeed that class which is totally opposed to all reified externalizations and all specializations of power. The proletariat is the bearer of a revolution that *can leave no other sphere of society untransformed*, that enforces the permanent domination of the past by the present and de- mands a universal critique of separation; the action of the proletariat must assume a form adequate to these tasks. No quantitative relief of its poverty, no illusory hierarchical incorporation, can supply a lasting cure for its dissatisfac- tion, for the proletariat cannot truly recognize itself in any particular wrong it has suffered; nor, therefore, *in the right- ing of any particular wrong* – nor even in the righting of many such wrongs; but only in the righting of the *unqual- ified* wrong that has been perpetrated upon it – the uni- versal wrong of its exclusion from life.

115 SIGNS OF A NEW and growing tendency toward negation proliferate in the more economically advanced countries. The spectacular system reacts to these signs with incom- prehension or attempts to misrepresent them, but they are sufficient proof that a new period has begun. After the failure of the working class's first subversive assault on cap-

italism, we are now witness to *the failure of capitalist abundance.* On the one hand, we see anti-union struggles of Western workers that have to be repressed (and repressed primarily by the unions themselves); at the same time rebellious tendencies among the young generate a protest that is still tentative and amorphous, yet already clearly embodies a rejection of the specialized sphere of the old politics, as well as of art and everyday life. These are two sides of the same coin, both signaling a new spontaneous struggle emerging under the sign of *criminality*, both portents of a second proletarian onslaught on class society. When the *enfants perdus* of this as-yet immobile horde enter once again upon the battlefield, which has changed yet stayed the same, a new General Ludd will be at their head – leading them this time in an onslaught on the *machinery of permitted consumption.*

116 THAT "LONG-SOUGHT political form whereby the economic emancipation of labor might finally be achieved" has taken on a clear outline in this century, in the shape of revolutionary workers' councils vesting all decision-making and executive powers in themselves and federating with one another through the exchange of delegates answerable to the base and recallable at any time. As yet such councils have enjoyed only a brief and experimental existence; their appearance has invariably occasioned attack and defeat by one or another of class society's means of defence – often including, it must be said, the presence of false consciousness within the councils themselves. As Pannekoek rightly stressed, the decision to set up workers'

councils does not in itself provide solutions so much as it "proposes problems." Yet the power of workers' councils is the one context in which the problems of the revolution of the proletariat can be truly solved. It is here that the objective preconditions of historical consciousness are assembled, opening the door to the realization of that active direct communication which marks the end of all specialization, all hierarchy, and all separation, and thanks to which existing conditions are transformed "into the conditions of unity." And it is here too that the proletarian subject can emerge from the struggle against a purely contemplative role, for consciousness is now equal to the practical organization that it has chosen for itself, and it has become inseparable from a coherent intervention in history.

117   ONCE EMBODIED IN the power of workers' councils – a power destined to supplant all other powers worldwide – the proletarian movement becomes its own product; this product is the producer himself, and in his own eyes the producer has himself as his goal. Only in this context can the spectacle's negation of life be negated in its turn.

118   THE APPEARANCE OF workers' councils during the first quarter of this century was the high point of the proletarian movement, but this reality has gone unnoticed, or else been presented in travestied form, because it inevitably vanished along with the remainder of a movement that the whole historical experience of the time tended to deny and destroy. From the standpoint of the renewal of the prole-

87

tariat's critical enterprise, however, the councils may be seen in their true light as the only undefeated aspect of a defeated movement: historical consciousness, aware that this is the only environment in which it can thrive, now perceives the councils as situated historically not at the periphery of an ebbing tide but rather at the center of a rising one.

119   A REVOLUTIONARY ORGANIZATION that exists before the establishment of the power of workers' councils – which must discover its own appropriate form through struggle – will know that, for all these historical reasons, it *cannot represent* the revolutionary class. It must simply recognize itself as radically separated from *the world of separation*.

120   THE REVOLUTIONARY ORGANIZATION is the coherent expression of the theory of praxis entering into two-way communication with practical struggles; it is thus part of the process of the coming into being of practical theory.

121   THE REVOLUTIONARY ORGANIZATION must necessarily constitute an integral critique of society – a critique, that is to say, which refuses to compromise with any form of separated power and which is directed globally against every aspect of alienated social life. In the revolutionary organization's struggle with class society, the weapons are nothing less than the *essence* of the antagonists themselves: the revolutionary organization cannot allow the conditions of division and hierarchy that obtain in the dominant society to be reproduced within itself. It must also fight con-

stantly against its own distortion by and within the reigning spectacle. The only restriction on individual participation in the revolutionary organization's total democracy is that imposed by the effective recognition and appropriation by each member of the coherence of the organization's critique, a coherence that must be borne out both in critical theory proper and in the relationship between that theory and practical activity.

122   As CAPITALISM'S ever-intensifying imposition of alienation at all levels makes it increasingly hard for workers to recognize and name their own impoverishment, and eventually puts them in the position of having either to reject it in its totality or do nothing at all, the revolutionary organization must learn that it can no longer *combat alienation by means of alienated forms of struggle*.

123   THE PROLETARIAN REVOLUTION is predicated entirely on the requirement that, for the first time, theory as the understanding of human practice be recognized and directly lived by the masses. This revolution demands that workers become dialecticians, and inscribe their thought upon practice; it thus asks much more of its *men without qualities* than the bourgeois revolution asked of those men with qualifications that it enlisted to run things (the partial ideological consciousness constructed by a segment of the bourgeois class had as its basis only a key *portion* of social life, namely the economy, where this class was *already in power*). It is thus the very evolution of class society into the spectacular organization of non-life that obliges the

89

revolutionary project to become *visibly* what it always was *in essence.*

124 REVOLUTIONARY THEORY is now the sworn enemy of all revolutionary ideology – *and it knows it.*

V

Time and History

O, gentlemen, the time of life is short!...
An if we live, we live to tread on kings.
— Shakespeare, *Henry IV*, Part I

125   MAN — THAT "NEGATIVE BEING who *is* solely to the extent that he abolishes being" — is one with time. Man's appropriation of his own nature is at the same time the apprehension of the unfolding of the universe. "History itself," says Marx, "is a *real* part of *natural history*, and of nature's becoming man." Conversely, the "natural history" in question exists effectively only through the process of a human history, through the development of the only agency capable of discovering this historical whole; one is reminded of a modern telescope, whose range enables it to track the retreat of nebulae *in time* toward the edge of the universe. History has always existed, but not always in its historical form. The temporalization of man, as effected through the mediation of a society, is equivalent to a humanization of time. The unconscious movement of time becomes manifest and *true* in historical consciousness.

126   THE MOVEMENT OF HISTORY properly so called (though *still hidden*) begins with the slow and imperceptible emergence of "the true nature of man," of that "nature which was born of human history — of the procreative act that gave rise to human society"; but society, even when it had mastered a technology and a language, and even though by then it was already the product of its own history, remained conscious only of a perpetual present. All knowledge, which was in any case limited by the memory of society's oldest members, was always borne by the *living*. Neither death nor reproduction were understood as governed by time. Time was motionless — a sort of enclosed space. When a more complex society did finally attain a

consciousness of time, its reaction was to deny rather than embrace it, for it viewed time not as something *passing*, but as something *returning*. This was a static type of society that organized time, true to its immediate experience of nature, on a *cyclical* model.

127 CYCLICAL TIME was already dominant in the experience of nomadic peoples, who confronted the same conditions at each moment of their roaming; as Hegel notes, "the wandering of nomads is a merely formal one, because it is limited to uniform spaces." Once a society became fixed in a locality, giving space content through the individualized development of specific areas, it found itself enclosed thereby within the location in question. A time-bound return to similar places thus gave way to the pure return of time in a single place, the repetition of a set of gestures. The shift from pastoralism to settled agriculture marked the end of an idle and contentless freedom, and the beginning of *labor*. The agrarian mode of production in general, governed by the rhythm of the seasons, was the basis of cyclical time in its fullest development. Eternity, as the return of the same here below, was *internal* to this time. Myth was the unified mental construct whose job it was to make sure that the whole cosmic order confirmed the order that this society had in fact already set up within its own frontiers.

128 THE SOCIAL APPROPRIATION of time and the production of man by means of human labor were developments that awaited the advent of a society divided into classes. The

power that built itself up on the basis of the penury of the society of cyclical time – the power, in other words, of the class which organized social labor therein and appropriated the limited surplus value to be extracted, also appropriated the *temporal surplus value* that resulted from its organization of social time; this class thus had sole possession of the irreversible time of the living. The only wealth that could exist in concentrated form in the sphere of power, there to be expended on extravagance and festivity, was also expended in the form of the squandering of *a historical time at society's surface*. The owners of this historical surplus value were the masters of the knowledge and enjoyment of directly experienced events. Separated off from the collective organization of time that predominated as a function of the repetitive form of production which was the basis of social life, historical time flowed independently above its own, static, community. This was the time of adventure, of war, the time in which the lords of cyclical society pursued their personal histories; the time too that emerged in clashes between communities foreign to one another – perturbations in society's unchanging order. For ordinary men, therefore, history sprang forth as an alien factor, as something they had not sought and against whose occurrence they had thought themselves secure. Yet this turning point also made possible the return of that negative human *restlessness* which had been at the origin of the whole (temporarily arrested) development.

129   IN ITS ESSENCE, cyclical time was a time without conflict. Yet even in this infancy of time, conflict was present: at

first, history struggled to become history through the practical activity of the masters. At a superficial level this history created irreversibility; its movement constituted the very time that it used up *within* the inexhaustible time of cyclical society.

130   SO-CALLED COLD SOCIETIES are societies that successfully slowed their participation in history down to the minimum, and maintained their conflicts with the natural and human environments, as well as their internal conflicts, in constant equilibrium. Although the vast diversity of institutions set up for this purpose bears eloquent testimony to the plasticity of human nature's self-creation, this testimony is of course only accessible to an outside observer, to an anthropologist *looking back* from within historical time. In each of these societies a definitive organizational structure ruled out change. The absolute conformity of their social practices, with which all human possibilities were exclusively and permanently identified, had no external limits except for the fear of falling into a formless animal condition. So, here, in order to remain human, men had to remain the same.

131   THE EMERGENCE OF political power, seemingly associated with the last great technical revolutions, such as iron smelting, which occurred at the threshold of a period that was to experience no further major upheavals until the rise of modern industry, also coincided with the first signs of the dissolution of the bonds of kinship. From this moment on, the succession of the generations left the natural realm

of the purely cyclical and became a purposeful succession of *events*, a mechanism for the transmission of power. Irreversible time was the prerogative of whoever ruled, and the prime yardstick of rulership lay in dynastic succession. The ruler's chief weapon was the written word, which now attained its full autonomous reality as mediation between consciousnesses. This independence, however, was indistinguishable from the general independence of a separate power as the mediation whereby society was constituted. With writing came a consciousness no longer conveyed and transmitted solely within the immediate relationships of the living – an *impersonal memory* that was the memory of the administration of society. "Writings are the thoughts of the State," said Novalis, "and archives are its memory."

132   AS THE EXPRESSION OF power's irreversible time, chronicles were a means of maintaining the voluntaristic forward progression of this time on the basis of the recording of its past; "voluntaristic," because such an orientation is bound to collapse, along with the particular power to which it corresponds, and sink once more into the indifferent oblivion of a solely cyclical time, a time known to the peasant masses who – no matter that empires may crumble along with their chronologies – never change. Those who *possessed history* gave it an orientation – a direction, and also a meaning. But their history unfolded and perished *apart*, as a sphere leaving the underlying society unaffected precisely because it was a sphere separate from common reality. This is why, from our point of view, the history of Oriental societies may be reduced to a history of religions:

all we can reconstruct from their ruins is the seemingly independent history of the illusions that once enveloped them. The masters who, protected by myth, enjoyed the *private ownership of history*, themselves did so at first in the realm of illusion. In China and Egypt, for example, they long held a monopoly on the immortality of the soul; likewise, their earliest officially recognized dynasties were an imaginary reconstruction of the past. Such illusory ownership by the masters, however, was at the same time the only ownership then possible both of the common history and of their own history. The expansion of their effective historical power went hand in hand with a vulgarization of this illusory-mythical ownership. All of these consequences flowed from the simple fact that it was only to the degree that the masters made it their task to furnish cyclical time with mythic underpinnings, as in the seasonal rites of the Chinese emperors, that they themselves were relatively emancipated therefrom.

133 THE DRY, UNEXPLAINED chronology which a deified authority offered to its subjects, and which was intended to be understood solely as the earthly execution of the commandments of myth, was destined to be transcended and to become conscious history. But, for this to happen, sizeable groups of people had first to experience real participation in history. From such practical communication between those who had *recognized one another* as possessors of a unique present, who had experienced the qualitative richness of events as their own activity, their own dwelling-place – in short, their own epoch – from such

communication arose the general language of historical communication. Those for whom irreversible time truly exists discover in it both the *memorable* and the *danger of forgetting*: "Herodotus of Halicarnassus here presents the results of his researches, that the great deeds of men may not be forgotten."

134   To REFLECT UPON HISTORY is also, inextricably, to re-flect upon power. Greece was that moment when power and changes in power were first debated and understood. This occurred under a *democracy of society's masters*, a sys-tem diametrically opposed to that of the despotic State, where power settled accounts only with itself, in the im-penetrable obscurity of its densest point, by means of *palace revolutions* whose outcome, whether success or fail-ure, invariably placed the event itself *beyond discussion*. The shared power of Greek communities inhered solely, however, in the *expending* of a social life whose *produc-tion* remained the separate and static domain of the slave class. The only people who lived were those who did not work. The divisions between Greek communities, and the struggle to exploit foreign cities, were the externalized expression of the principle of separation on which each of them was based internally. Greece, which dreamed of a universal history, was thus unable to unite in the face of invasion from without; it could not even manage to standardize the calendars of its constituent cities. Histor-ical time became conscious in Greece – but it was not yet conscious of itself.

135 THE REGRESSION OF Western thought that occurred once
the local conditions favoring the Greek communities had
disappeared was not accompanied by any reconstruction
of the old mythic structures. Clashes between Mediter-
ranean peoples and the constitution and collapse of the
Roman State gave rise instead to *semi-historical religions* that
were to become basic components of the new consciousness of time, and the new armature of separated power.

136 MONOTHEISTIC RELIGIONS were a compromise between
myth and history, between the cyclical time which still
dominated the sphere of production and the irreversible
time which was the theater of conflicts and realignments
between peoples. The religions that evolved out of Juda-
ism were the abstract universal recognition of an irreversible time now democratized, open to all, yet still confined
to the realm of illusion. Time remained entirely oriented
toward a single final event: "The Kingdom of God is at
hand." These religions had germinated and taken root in
the soil of history; even here, however, they maintained
a radical opposition to history. Semi-historical religion
established qualitative starting points in time – the birth
of Christ, the flight of Muhammad – yet its irreversible
time, introducing an effective accumulation which would
take the form of conquest in Islam and that of an increase
in capital in the Christianity of the Reformation, was in
fact inverted in religious thought, so as to become a sort of
countdown: the wait, as time ran out, for the Last Judgment,
for the moment of accession to the other, true world. Eternity emerged from cyclical time; it was that time's beyond.

Eternity was also what humbled time in its mere irreversible flow – suppressing history as history continued – by positioning itself *beyond irreversible time*, as a pure point which cyclical time would enter only to be abolished. As Bossuet could still say: "So, by way of the passing of time, we enter eternity, which does not pass."

137 THE MIDDLE AGES, an unfinished mythical world whose perfection lay outside itself, was the period when cyclical time, which still governed the major part of production, suffered history's first real gnawing inroads. A measure of irreversible time now became available to everyone individually, in the form of the successive stages of life, in the form of life apprehended as a voyage, a one-way passage through a world whose meaning was elsewhere. Thus the *pilgrim* was the man who emerged from cyclical time to become in actuality the traveler that each individual was qua sign. Personal historical life invariably found its fulfillment within power's orbit – either in struggles waged by power or in struggles in which power was disputed; yet power's irreversible time was now shared to an unlimited degree within the context of the general unity that the oriented time of the Christian era ensured. This was a world of *armed faith* in which the activity of the masters revolved around fealty and around challenges to fealty owed. Under the feudal regime born of the coming together of "the martial organization of the army during the actual conquest" and "the action of the productive forces found in the conquered countries" (*The German Ideology*) – and among the factors responsible for organizing

those productive forces must be included their religious language – under this regime social domination was divided up between the Church on the one hand and State power on the other, the latter being further broken down in accordance with the complex relations of suzerainty and vassalage characteristic, respectively, of rural landed property and urban communes. This diversification of possible historical life reflected the gradual emergence, following the collapse of the great official enterprise of this world, namely the Crusades, of the period's unseen contribution: a society carried along in its unconscious depths by irreversible time, the time directly experienced by the bourgeoisie in the production of commodities, the founding and expansion of the towns, the commercial discovery of the planet – in a word, the practical experimentation that obliterated any mythical organization of the cosmos once and for all.

138 As THE MIDDLE AGES came to an end, the irreversible time that had invaded society was experienced by a consciousness still attached to the old order as an obsession with death. This was the melancholy of a world passing away – the last world where the security of myth could still balance history; and for this melancholy all earthly things were inevitably embarked on the path of corruption. The great European peasant revolts were likewise a *response to history* – a history that was wresting the peasantry from the patriarchal slumber thitherto guaranteed by the feudal order. This was the moment when a millenarian utopianism aspiring to *build heaven on earth* brought back to

the forefront an idea that had been at the origin of semi-historical religion, when the early Christian communities, like the Judaic messianism from which they sprang, responded to the troubles and misfortunes of their time by announcing the imminent realization of God's Kingdom, and so added an element of disquiet and subversion to ancient society. The Christianity that later shared in imperial power denounced whatever remained of this hope as mere superstition: this is the meaning of the Augustinian pronouncement — the archetype of all the satisfecits of modern ideology — according to which the established Church was itself, and had long been, that self-same hoped-for kingdom. The social revolt of the millenarian peasantry naturally defined itself as an attempt to overthrow the Church. Millenarianism unfolded, however, in a historical world — not in the realm of myth. So, contrary to what Norman Cohn believes he has demonstrated in *The Pursuit of the Millennium*, modern revolutionary hopes are not an irrational sequel to the religious passion of millenarianism. The exact opposite is true: millenarianism, the expression of a revolutionary class struggle speaking the language of religion for the last time, was already a modern revolutionary tendency, lacking only the consciousness of being *historical and nothing more*. The millenarians were doomed to defeat because they could not recognize revolution as their own handiwork. The fact that they made their action conditional upon an external sign of God's will was a translation onto the level of thought of the tendency of insurgent peasants to follow outside leaders. The peasant class could achieve a clear consciousness neither of the workings of society nor of the way to conduct its own struggle, and it was because it lacked these prerequisites of unity in its action and consciousness that the peasantry formulated its project and waged its wars according to the imagery of an earthly paradise.

139 THE RENAISSANCE EMBODIED the new form of possession of historical life. Seeking its heritage and its juridical basis in Antiquity, it was the bearer of a joyous break with eternity. The irreversible time of the Renaissance was that of an infinite accumulation of knowledge, while the historical consciousness generated by the experience of democratic communities, as of the effects of those forces that had brought on their ruin, was now, with Machiavelli, able to resume its reflection upon secular power, and say the unsayable about the State. In the exuberant life of the Italian cities, in the arts of festival, life came to recognize itself as the enjoyment of the passing of time. But this enjoyment of transience would turn out to be transient itself. The song of Lorenzo de' Medici, which Burckhardt considered "the very spirit of the Renaissance," is the eulogy delivered upon itself by this fragile historical feast: "*Quant' è bella giovinezza / Che si fugge tuttavia.*"

140 THE TIRELESS PURSUIT of a monopoly of historical life by the absolute-monarchist State, a transitional form along the way to complete domination by the bourgeois class, clearly illuminates the highest expression of the bourgeoisie's new irreversible time. The time with which the bourgeoisie was inextricably bound up was *labor-time*, now at

last emancipated from the cyclical realm. With the rise of the bourgeoisie, work became *that work which transforms historical conditions*. The bourgeoisie was the first ruling class for which labor was a value. By abolishing all social privilege, and by recognizing no value unrelated to the exploitation of labor, the bourgeoisie effectively conflated its own value qua ruling class with labor, and made the progress of labor the only measure of its own progress. The class that accumulated commodities and capital continually modified nature by modifying labor itself – by unleashing labor's productivity. All social life was by this time concentrated in the ornamented poverty of the Court – in the chintzy trappings of a bleak State administration whose apex was the "profession of king"; and all individual historical freedom had had to consent to this sacrifice. The free play of the feudal lords' irreversible time had exhausted itself in their last, lost battles: in the Fronde, or in the Scots' uprising in support of Charles Edward. The world had a new foundation.

141 THE VICTORY OF the bourgeoisie was the victory of a *profoundly historical* time – the time corresponding to the economic form of production, which transformed society permanently, and from top to bottom. So long as agriculture was the chief type of labor, cyclical time retained its deep-down hold over society and tended to nourish those combined forces of tradition which slowed down the movement of history. But the irreversible time of the bourgeois economic revolution eliminated all such vestiges throughout the world. History, which had hitherto appeared to

express nothing more than the activity of individual members of the ruling class, and had thus been conceived of as a chronology of events, was now perceived in its *general movement* – an inexorable movement that crushed individuals before it. By discovering its basis in political economy, history became aware of the existence of what had been its unconscious. This unconscious, however, continued to exist as such – and history still could not draw it out into the full light of day. This blind prehistory, a new fatality that no one controls, is the only thing that the commodity economy has democratized.

142 THOUGH EVER-PRESENT in society's depths, history tended to be invisible at its surface. The triumph of irreversible time was also its metamorphosis into the *time of things*, because the weapon that had ensured its victory was, precisely, the mass production of objects in accordance with the laws of the commodity. The main product that economic development transformed from a luxurious rarity to a commonly consumed item was thus history itself – but only in the form of the history of that abstract movement which dominated any qualitative use of life. Whereas the cyclical time of an earlier era had supported an ever-increasing measure of historical time lived by individuals and groups, irreversible time's reign over production would tend socially to eliminate all such lived time.

143 SO THE BOURGEOISIE UNVEILED irreversible historical time and imposed it on society only to deprive society of its *use*. Once there was history, but "there is no longer any

history" – because the class of owners of the economy, who cannot break with *economic history*, must repress any other use of irreversible time as representing an immediate threat to itself. The ruling class, made up of *specialists in the ownership of things* who for that very reason are themselves owned by things, is obliged to tie its fate to the maintenance of a reified history and to the permanent preservation of a new historical immobility. Meanwhile the worker, at the base of society, is for the first time not materially *estranged from history*, for now the irreversible is generated from below. By demanding to *live* the historical time that it creates, the proletariat discovers the simple, unforgettable core of its revolutionary project; and every attempt to carry this project through – though all up to now have gone down to defeat – signals a possible point of departure for a new historical life.

144   THE IRREVERSIBLE TIME of a bourgeoisie that had just seized power was called by its own name, and assigned an absolute origin: Year One of the Republic. But the revolutionary ideology of generalized freedom that had served to overthrow the last relics of a myth-based ordering of values, along with all traditional forms of social organization, was already unable completely to conceal the real goal that it had thus draped in Roman costume – namely, generalized *freedom of trade*. The society of the commodity, soon discovering that it must reinstate the passivity which it had to shake to its foundations in order to inaugurate its own unchallenged rule, now found that, for its purposes, "Christianity with its religious cult of man in the abstract

was the most fitting form of religion" (*Capital*). So the bourgeoisie concluded a pact with this religion, an arrangement reflected in its presentation of time: the Revolutionary calendar was abandoned and irreversible time was returned to the straitjacket of a duly extended Christian Era.

145 THE DEVELOPMENT OF capitalism meant the unification of irreversible time *on a world scale*. Universal history became a reality because the entire globe was brought under the sway of this time's progression. But a history that is thus the same everywhere at once has as yet amounted to nothing more than an intrahistorical refusal of history. What appears the world over as *the same day* is merely the time of economic production – time cut up into equal abstract fragments. Unified irreversible time still belongs to the world market – and, by extension, to the world spectacle.

146 THE IRREVERSIBLE TIME of production is first and foremost the measure of commodities. The time officially promoted all around the world as the *general time of society*, since it signifies nothing beyond those special interests which constitute it, is therefore not general in character, but *particular*.

VI

Spectacular Time

We have nothing that is ours except time, which even those without a roof can enjoy.

— Baltasar Gracián, *Oráculo manual y Arte de prudencia*

147 THE TIME OF PRODUCTION, time-as-commodity, is an infinite accumulation of equivalent intervals. It is irreversible time made abstract: each segment must demonstrate by the clock its purely quantitative equality with all other segments. This time manifests nothing in its effective reality aside from its *exchangeability*. It is under the rule of time-as-commodity that "time is everything, man is nothing; he is at the most time's carcass" (*The Poverty of Philosophy*). This is time devalued — the complete inversion of time as "the sphere of human development."

148 THE GENERAL TIME of human non-development also has a complementary aspect, that of a *consumable time* which, on the basis of a determinate form of production, presents itself in the everyday life of society as a *pseudo-cyclical time*.

149 PSEUDO-CYCLICAL TIME is in fact merely the *consumable disguise* of the time-as-commodity of the production system, and it exhibits the essential traits of that time: homogeneous and exchangeable units, and the suppression of any qualitative dimension. But as a by-product of time-as-commodity intended to promote and maintain the backwardness of everyday life it necessarily finds itself laden with false attributions of value, and it must manifest itself as a succession of artificially distinct moments.

150 PSEUDO-CYCLICAL TIME typifies the consumption of modern economic survival — of that augmented survival in which daily lived experience embodies no free choices and is subject, no longer to the natural order, but to a pseudo-nature

constructed by means of alienated labor. It is therefore quite "natural" that pseudo-cyclical time should echo the old cyclical rhythms that governed survival in pre-industrial societies. It builds, in fact, on the natural vestiges of cyclical time, while also using these as models on which to base new but homologous variants: day and night, weekly work and weekly rest, the cycle of vacations and so on.

151 PSEUDO-CYCLICAL TIME is a time *transformed by industry.* The time founded on commodity production is itself a consumable commodity, recombining everything which, during the period of the old unitary society's disintegration, had become distinct: private life, economic life, political life. The entirety of the consumable time of modern society ends up being treated as raw material for the production of a diversity of new products to be put on the market as socially controlled uses of time. "A product, though ready for immediate consumption, may nevertheless serve as raw material for a further product" (*Capital*).

152 IN ITS MOST ADVANCED sectors, a highly concentrated capitalism has begun selling "fully equipped" blocks of time, each of which is a complete commodity combining a variety of other commodities. This is the logic behind the appearance, within an expanding economy of "services" and leisure activities, of the "all-inclusive" purchase of spectacular forms of housing, of collective pseudo-travel, of participation in cultural consumption and even of sociability itself, in the form of "exciting conversations," "meetings with celebrities" and suchlike. Spectacular

commodities of this type could obviously not exist were it not for the increasing impoverishment of the realities they parody. And, not surprisingly, they are also paradigmatic of modern sales techniques in that they may be bought on credit.

153 CONSUMABLE PSEUDO-CYCLICAL TIME is the time of the spectacle: in the narrow sense, as the time appropriate to the consumption of images, and, in the broadest sense, as the image of the consumption of time. The time appropriate to the consumption of images, the medium of all commodities, is at once the chosen field of operations of the mechanisms of the spectacle and the goal that these mechanisms hold up overall as the locus and central representation of every individual act of consumption; as we know, modern society's obsession with *saving time*, whether by means of faster transport or by means of powdered soup, has the positive result that the average American spends three to six hours daily watching television. The social image of the consumption of time is for its part exclusively dominated by leisure time and vacations – moments portrayed, like all spectacular commodities, *at a distance*, and as desirable by definition. This particular commodity is explicitly presented as a moment of authentic life whose cyclical return we are supposed to look forward to. Yet even in such special moments, ostensibly moments of *life*, the only thing being generated, the only thing to be seen and reproduced, is the spectacle – albeit at a higher-than-usual level of intensity. And what has been passed off as authentic life turns out to be merely a life more *authentically spectacular.*

154   OUR EPOCH, WHICH PRESENTS its time to itself as essentially made up of many frequently recurring festivities, is
actually an epoch without festival. Those moments when,
under the reign of cyclical time, the community would
participate in a luxurious expenditure of life, are strictly
unavailable to a society where neither community nor
luxury exists. Mass pseudo-festivals, with their travesty of
dialogue and their parody of the gift, may incite people
to excessive spending, but they produce only a disillu-
sion – which is invariably in turn offset by further false
promises. The self-approbation of the time of modern survival can only be reinforced, in the spectacle, by reduction in its use value. The reality of time has been replaced
by its *publicity*.

155   IN ANCIENT SOCIETIES the consumption of cyclical time
was consistent with the actual labor of those societies.
By contrast, the consumption of pseudo-cyclical time in
developed economies is at odds with the abstract irreversible time implicit in their system of production. Cyclical
time was the time of a motionless illusion authentically
experienced; spectacular time is the time of a real transformation experienced as illusion.

156   INNOVATION IS EVER PRESENT in the process of the production of things. This is not true of consumption, which
is never anything but more of the same. Because dead labor
continues to dominate living labor, in spectacular time the
past continues to dominate the present.

113

157 ANOTHER ASPECT OF the lack of historical life in general is that the individual life is still not historical. The pseudo-events that vie for attention in the spectacle's dramatizations have not been lived by those who are thus informed about them. In any case they are quickly forgotten, thanks to the precipitation with which the spectacle's pulsing machinery replaces one by the next. At the same time, everything really lived has no relation to society's official version of irreversible time, and is directly opposed to the pseudo-cyclical rhythm of that time's consumable by-products. Such individual lived experience of a cut-off everyday life remains bereft of language or concept, and it lacks any critical access to its own antecedents, which are nowhere recorded. It cannot be communicated. And it is misunderstood and forgotten to the benefit of the spectacle's false memory of the unmemorable.

158 THE SPECTACLE, BEING the reigning social organization of a paralyzed history, of a paralyzed memory, of an abandonment of any history founded in historical time, is in effect a *false consciousness of time*.

159 A PREREQUISITE TO the enrollment of the workers as "free" producers and consumers of time-as-commodity was the *violent expropriation of their time*. The spectacular restoration of time was only possible on the basis of this initial dispossession of the producers.

160 THE IRREDUCIBLY BIOLOGICAL element that labor retains – evident as much in our dependence on the natural

cycle of sleeping and waking as in the marks of a lifetime's wear and tear, which attest to the irreversible time of the individual – is treated by the modern production system as a strictly secondary consideration. Such factors are consequently ignored in the official discourse of this system as it advances, and as it generates the consumable trophies that translate its triumphant forward march into accessible terms. Immobilized at the distorted center of the movement of its world, the consciousness of the spectator can have no sense of an individual life moving toward self-realization, or toward death. Someone who has given up the idea of living life will surely never be able to embrace death. Promoters of life insurance merely intimate that it is reprehensible to die without first arranging for the system's adjustment to the economic loss one's death will incur; and the promoters of the "American way of death" dwell solely on how much of the *appearance* of life can be maintained in the individual's encounter with death. Elsewhere under advertising's bombardments it is simply forbidden to get old. Anybody and everybody is urged to economize on an alleged "capital of youth" – which, though it is unlikely to have suffered much in the way of dilapidation, has scant prospect of ever attaining the durable and cumulative properties of capital *tout court*. This social absence of death is one with the social absence of life.

161   As HEGEL SHOWED, time is a *necessary* alienation, being the medium in which the subject realizes himself while losing himself, becomes other in order to become truly

himself. The opposite obtains in the case of the alienation that now holds sway — the alienation suffered by the producers of an *estranged present*. This is a *spatial alienation*, whereby a society which radically severs the subject from the activity that it steals from him separates him in the first place from his own time. Social alienation, though in principle surmountable, is nevertheless the alienation that has forbidden and petrified the possibilities and risks of a *living* alienation within time.

162 IN CONTRAST TO the passing *fashions* that clash and fuse on the frivolous surface of a contemplated pseudo-cyclical time, the *grand style* of our era can ever be recognized in whatever is governed by the obvious yet carefully concealed necessity for revolution.

163 TIME'S NATURAL BASIS, the sensory data of its passage, becomes human and social inasmuch as it exists *for human beings*. The limitations of human practice, and the various stages of labor — these are what until now have humanized (and also dehumanized) time, both cyclical time and the separated irreversible time of the economic system of production. The revolutionary project of a classless society, of a generalized historical life, is also the project of a withering away of the social measurement of time in favor of an individual and collective irreversible time which is playful in character and which encompasses, simultaneously present within it, a variety of autonomous yet effectively federated times — the complete realization, in short, within the medium of time, of that commun-

ism which "abolishes everything that exists independently of individuals."

164 THE WORLD ALREADY has the dream of a such a time; it has yet to come into possession of the consciousness that will allow it to experience its reality.

VII

ENVIRONMENTAL PLANNING

And he who becomes master of a city used to being free and does not destroy her can expect to be destroyed by her, because always she has as pretext in rebellion the name of liberty and her old customs, which never through either length of time or benefits are forgotten, and in spite of anything that can be done or foreseen, unless citizens are disunited or dispersed, they do not forget that name and those institutions....

— Machiavelli, *The Prince*

165 THE CAPITALIST PRODUCTION system has unified space, breaking down the boundaries between one society and the next. This unification is also a process, at once extensive and intensive, of *trivialization*. Just as the accumulation of commodities mass-produced for the abstract space of the market inevitably shattered all regional and legal barriers, as well as all those corporative restrictions that served in the Middle Ages to preserve the quality of craft production, so too it was bound to dissipate the independence and quality of *places*. The power to homogenize is the heavy artillery that has battered down all Chinese walls.

166 IF HENCEFORWARD the *free space of commodities* is subject at every moment to modification and reconstruction, this is so that it may become ever more identical to itself, and achieve as nearly as possible a perfectly static monotony.

167 THIS SOCIETY ELIMINATES geographical distance only to reap distance internally in the form of spectacular separation.

168 HUMAN CIRCULATION considered as something to be consumed — tourism — is a by-product of the circulation of commodities; basically, tourism is the chance to go and see what has been made trite. The economic management of travel to different places suffices in itself to ensure those places' interchangeability. The same modernization that has deprived travel of its temporal aspect has likewise deprived it of the reality of space.

169   A SOCIETY THAT molds its entire surroundings has necessarily evolved its own techniques for working on the material basis of this set of tasks. That material basis is the
society's actual *territory*. Urbanism is the mode of appropriation of the natural and human environment by capitalism,
which, true to its logical development toward absolute
domination, can (and now must) refashion the totality of
space into *its own peculiar decor*.

170   THE REQUIREMENT OF capitalism that is met by urbanism in the form of a freezing of life might be described,
in Hegelian terms, as an absolute predominance of "tran-
quil side-by-sideness" in space over "restless becoming in
the progression of time."

171   IT IS TRUE THAT all the capitalist economy's technical
forces should be understood as effecting separations, but
in the case of urbanism we are dealing with the fitting
out of the general basis of those forces, with the readying
of the ground in preparation for their deployment – in a
word, with the technology of *separation itself*.

172   URBANISM IS THE MODERN way of tackling the ongoing
need to safeguard class power by ensuring the atomization
of workers dangerously *massed together* by the conditions
of urban production. The unremitting struggle that has
had to be waged against the possibility of workers coming together in whatever manner has found a perfect field
of action in urbanism. The effort of all established powers, since the experience of the French Revolution, to

augment their means of keeping order in the street has eventually culminated in the suppression of the street itself. Evoking a "civilization...moving along a one-way road," Lewis Mumford, in *The City in History*, points out that with the advent of long-distance mass communications, the isolation of the population has become a much more effective means of control. But the general trend toward isolation, which is the essential reality of urbanism, must also embody a controlled reintegration of the workers based on the planned needs of production and consumption. Such an integration into the system must recapture isolated individuals as individuals *isolated together*. Factories and cultural centers, holiday camps and housing developments – all are expressly oriented to the goals of a pseudo-community of this kind. These imperatives pursue the isolated individual right into the *family cell*, where the generalized use of receivers of the spectacle's message ensures that his isolation is filled with the dominant images – images that indeed attain their full force only by virtue of this isolation.

173 IN ALL PREVIOUS PERIODS, architectural innovation served the ruling class exclusively; now for the first time there is such a thing as a new architecture specifically for the poor. Both formal poverty and the immense extension of this new experience in housing are the result of its *mass* character, dictated at once by its ultimate ends and by the modern conditions of construction. At the core of these conditions we naturally find an *authoritarian decision-making process* that abstractly develops any environment into

an environment of abstraction. The same architecture appears everywhere just as soon as industrialization begins, even in the countries that are the furthest behind in this regard, for even these are considered a fertile terrain for the implantation of the new type of social existence. The threshold crossed in the growth of society's material power, and the corresponding *lag* in the conscious appropriation of this power, are just as clearly manifested in urbanism as they are, say, in the spheres of nuclear weapons or of the management of births (where the possibility of manipulated heredity is already on the horizon).

174 WE ALREADY LIVE in the era of the self-destruction of the urban environment. The explosion of cities into the countryside, covering it with what Mumford calls "formless masses" of urban debris, is presided over in unmediated fashion by the requirements of consumption. The dictatorship of the automobile, the pilot product of the first stage of commodity abundance, has left its mark on the landscape in the dominance of freeways that bypass the old urban centers and promote an ever greater dispersal. Meanwhile, instants of incomplete reorganization of the urban fabric briefly crystallize around the "distribution factories" – giant shopping centers created *ex nihilo* and surrounded by acres of parking space; but even these temples of frenetic consumption are subject to the irresistible centrifugal trend, and when, as partial reconstructions of the city, they in turn become overtaxed secondary centers, they are likewise cast aside. The technical organization of consumption is thus merely the herald of that

general process of dissolution which brings the city to the point where *it consumes itself.*

175　THE HISTORY OF the economy, whose development has turned entirely on the opposition between town and country, has progressed so far that it has now succeeded in abolishing both of these poles. The present *paralysis* of overall historical development, due to the exclusive pursuit of the economy's independent goals, means that the moment when town and country begin to disappear, so far from marking the transcendence of the split between them, marks instead their simultaneous collapse. The reciprocal erosion of town and country that has resulted from the faltering of the historical movement by whose means existing urban reality should have been superseded is clearly reflected in the bits and pieces of both that are strewn across the most advanced portions of the industrialized world.

176　UNIVERSAL HISTORY WAS BORN in cities, and attained its majority with the town's decisive victory over the country. Marx considered that one of the bourgeoisie's great merits as a revolutionary class was the fact that it "subjected the country to the rule of the towns" – whose very air made one free. But while the history of cities is certainly a history of freedom, it is also a history of tyranny, of State administration controlling not only the country but also the city itself. The towns may have supplied the historical battleground for the struggle for freedom, but up to now they have not taken possession of that freedom.

The city is the *locus of history* because it embodies at once a concentration of social power, which is what makes the historical enterprise possible, and a consciousness of the past. The present urge to destroy cities is thus merely another index of the belatedness of the economy's subordination to historical consciousness, the tardiness of a unification that will enable society to recapture its alienated powers.

177   "THE COUNTRY DEMONSTRATES just the opposite fact – isolation and separation" (*The German Ideology*). As it destroys the cities, urbanism institutes a *pseudo-countryside* devoid not only of the natural relationships of the country of former times but also of the direct (and directly contested) relationships of the historical cities. The forms of habitation and the spectacular control of today's "planned environment" have created a new, artificial peasantry. The geographic dispersal and narrow-mindedness that always prevented the peasantry from undertaking independent action and becoming a creative historical force are equally characteristic of these modern producers, for whom the movement of a world of their own making is every bit as inaccessible as were the natural rhythms of work for an earlier agrarian society. The traditional peasantry was the unshakeable basis of "Oriental despotism," and its very scatteredness *called forth* bureaucratic centralization; the new peasantry that has emerged as the product of the growth of modern state bureaucracy differs from the old in that its *apathy* has had to be *historically manufactured* and maintained: natural ignorance has given way to the organ-

ized spectacle of error. The "new towns" of the technological pseudo-peasantry are the clearest of indications,
inscribed on the land, of the break with historical time on
which they are founded; their motto might well be: "On
this spot nothing will ever happen – and *nothing ever has*."
Quite obviously, it is precisely because the liberation of
history, which must take place in the cities, has not yet
occurred, that the forces of *historical absence* have set about
designing their own exclusive landscape there.

178 THE SAME HISTORY that threatens this twilight world is
capable of subjecting space to a directly experienced time.
The proletarian revolution is that *critique of human geogra-
phy* whereby individuals and communities must construct
places and events commensurate with the appropriation,
no longer just of their labor, but of their total history.
By virtue of the resulting mobile space of play, and by virtue of freely chosen variations in the rules of the game,
the independence of places will be rediscovered without
any new exclusive tie to the soil, and thus too the authentic *journey* will be restored to us, along with authentic
life understood as a journey containing its whole meaning within itself.

179 THE MOST REVOLUTIONARY IDEA concerning city plan-
ning derives neither from urbanism, nor from technology,
nor from aesthetics. I refer to the decision to reconstruct
the entire environment in accordance with the needs of
the power of established workers' councils – the needs,
in other words, of the anti-State dictatorship of the prole-

tariat, the needs of *dialogue* invested with executive power. The power of workers' councils can be effective only if it transforms the totality of existing conditions, and it cannot assign itself any lesser a task if it aspires to be recognized – and *to recognize itself* – in a world of its own design.

VIII

NEGATION AND CONSUMPTION

IN THE CULTURAL SPHERE

*Do you seriously think we shall live long enough to see a political revolu-
tion? — we, the contemporaries of these Germans? My friend, you believe
what you want to believe.... Let us judge Germany on the basis of its present history — and surely you are not going to object that all its history is
falsified, or that all its present public life does not reflect the actual state of
the people? Read whatever papers you please, and you cannot fail to be con-
vinced that we never stop (and you must concede that the censorship pre-
vents no one from stopping) celebrating the freedom and national happiness
that we enjoy....*

— Ruge to Marx, March 1843

180 CULTURE IS THE GENERAL sphere of knowledge, and of representations of lived experience, within a historical society divided into classes; what this amounts to is that culture is the power to generalize, existing *apart*, as an intellectual division of labor and as the intellectual labor of division. Culture detached itself from the unity of myth-based society, according to Hegel, "when the power to unify disappeared from the life of man, and opposites lost their connection and living interaction, and became autonomous" ("The Difference between the Philosophical Systems of Fichte and Schelling"). In thus gaining its independence, culture was embarked on an imperialistic career of self-enrichment that was at the same time the beginning of the decline of its independence. The history that brought culture's relative autonomy into being, along with ideological illusions concerning that autonomy, is also expressed as the history of culture. And the whole triumphant history of culture can be understood as the history of the revelation of culture's insufficiency, as a march toward culture's self-abolition. Culture is the locus of the search for lost unity. In the course of this search, culture as a separate sphere is obliged to negate itself.

181 THE STRUGGLE BETWEEN tradition and innovation, which is the basic principle of the internal development of the culture of historical societies, is predicated entirely on the permanent victory of innovation. Cultural innovation is impelled solely, however, by that total historical movement which, by becoming conscious of its totality, tends

toward the transcendence of its own cultural presupposi-
tions – and hence toward the suppression of all separations.

182   THE SUDDEN EXPANSION of society's knowledge, including – as the heart of culture – an understanding of history,
brought about the irreversible self-knowledge that found
expression in the abolition of God. This "prerequisite of
every critique," however, was also the first task of a critique without end. In a situation where there are no longer
any tenable rules of action, culture's every *result* propels
it toward its own dissolution. Just like philosophy the
moment it achieved its full independence, every discipline,
once it becomes autonomous, is bound to collapse – in
the first place as an attempt to offer a coherent account
of the social totality, and eventually even as a partial methodology viable within its own domain. The *lack of rationality* in a separated culture is what dooms it to disappear,
for that culture itself embodies a call for the victory of
the rational.

183   CULTURE ISSUED FROM a history that had dissolved the
way of life of the old world, yet culture as a separate sphere
is as yet no more than an intelligence and a sensory communication which, in a *partially historical* society, must
themselves remain partial. Culture is the meaning of an
insufficiently meaningful world.

184   THE END OF THE HISTORY of culture manifests itself
under two antagonistic aspects: the project of culture's
self-transcendence as part of total history, and its manage-

ment as a dead thing to be contemplated in the spectacle. The first tendency has cast its lot with the critique of society, the second with the defense of class power.

185 EACH OF THE TWO aspects of the end of culture has a unitary existence, as much in all spheres of knowledge as in all spheres of sensory representation – that is, in all spheres of what was formerly understood as *art* in the most general sense. The first aspect enshrines an opposition between, on the one hand, the accumulation of a fragmentary knowledge which becomes useless in that any endorsement of existing conditions must eventually entail a rejection of *that knowlege itself*, and, on the other hand, the theory of practice, which alone has access, not only to the truth of all the knowledge in question, but also to the secret of its use. The second aspect enshrines an opposition between the critical self-destruction of society's old *common language* and its artificial reconstruction, within the commodity spectacle, as the illusory representation of non-life.

186 ONCE SOCIETY HAS LOST the community that myth was formerly able to ensure, it must inevitably lose all the reference points of a truly common language until such time as the divided character of an inactive community is superseded by the inauguration of a real historical community. As soon as art – which constituted that former common language of social inaction – establishes itself as independent in the modern sense, emerging from its first, religious universe to become the individual production of separate

works, it becomes subject, as one instance among others, to the movement governing the history of the whole of culture as a separated realm. Art's declaration of independence is thus the beginning of the end of art.

187 THE FACT THAT the language of real communication has been lost is what the modern movement of art's decay, and ultimately of its formal annihilation, expresses *positively*. What it expresses *negatively* is that a new common language has yet to be found — not, this time, in the form of unilaterally arrived-at conclusions like those which, from the viewpoint of historical art, *always came on the scene too late*, speaking *to others* of what had been experienced without any real dialogue, and accepting this shortfall of life as inevitable — but rather in a praxis embodying both an unmediated activity and a language commensurate with it. The point is to take effective possession of the community of dialogue, and the playful relationship to time, which the works of the poets and artists have heretofore merely *represented*.

188 WHEN A NEWLY INDEPENDENT art paints its world in brilliant colors, then a moment of life has grown old. By art's brilliant colors it cannot be rejuvenated but only recalled to mind. The greatness of art makes its appearance only as dusk begins to fall over life.

189 THE HISTORICAL TIME that invaded art in fact found its first expression in the artistic sphere, beginning with the baroque. Baroque was the art of a world that had lost its

center with the demise of the last mythic order recognized by the Middle Ages, an order founded, both cosmically and from the point of view of earthly government, on the unity between Christianity and the ghost of an Empire. An *art of change* was obliged to embody the principle of the ephemeral that it recognized in the world. In the words of Eugenio d'Ors, it chose "life as opposed to eternity." Theater and festival, or theatrical festival – these were the essential moments of the baroque, moments wherein all specific artistic expression derived its meaning from its reference to the decor of a constructed space, to a construction that had to constitute its own unifying center; and that center was *passage*, inscribed as a vulnerable equilibrium on an overall dynamic disorder. The sometimes excessive importance taken on in modern discussions of aesthetics by the concept of the baroque reflects a growing awareness of the impossibility of classicism in art: for three centuries all efforts to create a normative classicism or neoclassicism have never been more than brief, artificial projects giving voice to the official discourse of the State – whether the State of the absolute monarchy or that of the revolutionary bourgeoisie draped in Roman togas. What eventually followed the baroque, once it had run its course, was an ever more individualistic art of negation which, from romanticism to cubism, renewed its assault time after time until the fragmentation and destruction of the artistic sphere were complete. The disappearance of a historical art, which was tied to the internal communications of an elite whose semi-independent social basis lay in the relatively playful conditions still directly experienced by the last aristocracies, also testified to the fact that capitalism had thrown up the first class power self-admittedly bereft of any ontological quality; a power whose foundation in the mere running of the economy bespoke the loss of all human *mastery*. The baroque ensemble, a unity itself long lost to the world of artistic creation, recurs in a certain sense in today's *consumption* of the entirety of the art of the past. The historical knowledge and recognition of all past art, along with its retrospective promotion to the rank of world art, serve to relativize it within the context of a global disorder which in turn constitutes a baroque edifice at a higher level, an edifice into which even the production of a baroque art, and all its possible revivals, is bound to be melded. The very fact that such "recollections" of the history of art should have become possible amounts to the *end of the world of art*. Only in this era of museums, when no artistic communication remains possible, can each and every earlier moment of art be accepted – and accepted as *equal in value* – for none, in view of the disappearance of the prerequisites of communication *in general*, suffers any longer from the disappearance of its own *particular* ability to communicate.

190 ART IN THE PERIOD of its dissolution, as a movement of negation in pursuit of its own transcendence in a historical society where history is not yet directly lived, is at once an art of change and a pure expression of the impossibility of change. The more grandiose its demands, the futher from its grasp is true self-realization. This is an art that is necessarily *avant-garde*; and it is an art that *is not*. Its vanguard is its own disappearance.

191 THE TWO CURRENTS that marked the end of modern art were dadaism and surrealism. Though they were only partially conscious of it, they paralleled the proletarian revolutionary movement's last great offensive; and the halting of that movement, which left them trapped within the very artistic sphere that they had declared dead and buried, was the fundamental cause of their own immobilization. Historically, dadaism and surrealism are at once bound up with one another and at odds with one another. This antagonism, involvement in which constituted for each of these movements the most consistent and radical aspect of its contribution, also attested to the internal deficiency in each's critique – namely, in both cases, a fatal one-sidedness. For dadaism sought *to abolish art without realizing it*, and surrealism sought *to realize art without abolishing it*. The critical position since worked out by the situationists demonstrates that the abolition and the realization of art are inseparable aspects of a single transcendence of art.

192 SPECTACULAR CONSUMPTION preserves the old culture in congealed form, going so far as to recuperate and rediffuse even its negative manifestations; in this way, the spectacle's cultural sector gives overt expression to what the spectacle is implicitly in its totality – *the communication of the incommunicable*. Thoroughgoing attacks on language are liable to emerge in this context coolly invested with positive value by the official world, for the aim is to promote reconciliation with a dominant state of things from which all communication has been triumphantly declared absent. Naturally, the critical truth of such attacks, as

utterances of the real life of modern poetry and art, is concealed. The spectacle, whose function it is *to bury history in culture*, presses the pseudo-novelty of its modernist means into the service of a strategy that defines it in the profoundest sense. Thus a school of neo-literature baldly admitting that it merely contemplates the written word for its own sake can pass itself off as something truly new. Meanwhile, beyond the unadorned claim that the dissolution of the communicable has a beauty all its own, one encounters the most modern tendency of spectacular culture – and the one most closely bound up with the repressive practice of the general social organization – seeking by means of a "global approach" to reconstruct a complex neo-artistic environment out of flotsam and jetsam; a good example of this is urbanism's striving to incorporate old scraps of art or hybrid aesthetico-technological forms. All of which shows how a general project of advanced capitalism is translated onto the plane of spectacular pseudo-culture – that project being the remolding of the fragmented worker into "a personality well integrated into the group" (cf. recent American sociology – Riesman, Whyte, et al.). Wherever one looks, one encounters this same intent: to *restructure society without community.*

193   A CULTURE NOW wholly commodity was bound to become the star commodity of the society of the spectacle. Clark Kerr, an ideologue at the cutting edge of this trend, reckons that the whole complex system of production, distribution and consumption of *knowledge* is already equivalent to 29 percent of the annual gross national product of

the United States, and he predicts that in the second half of this century culture will become the driving force of the American economy, so assuming the role of the automobile industry in the first half, or that of the railroads in the late nineteenth century.

194 THE TASK OF the complex of claims still evolving as *spectacular thought* is to justify a society with no justification, and ultimately to establish itself as a general science of false consciousness. This thought is entirely determined by the fact that it cannot and does not wish to apprehend its own material foundation in the spectacular system.

195 THE OFFICIAL THOUGHT of the social organization of appearances is itself obscured by the generalized *subcommunication* that it has to defend. It does not see that conflict is at the root of every feature of its universe. Spectacular power, which is absolute within the unchallengeable internal logic of the spectacle's language, corrupts its specialists absolutely. They are corrupted by their experience of contempt, and by the success of that contempt, for the contempt they feel is confirmed by their acquaintanceship with that genuinely *contemptible individual* – the spectator.

196 A NEW DIVISION of tasks occurs within the specialized thought of the spectacular system in response to the new problems presented by the perfecting of this system itself: in the first place modern sociology undertakes a *spectacular critique of the spectacle*, studying separation with the sole aid of separation's own conceptual and material tools;

meanwhile, from within the various disciplines in which structuralism has taken root, an apologetics of the spectacle is disseminated as the thought of non-thought, as an authorized amnesia with respect to historical practice. As forms of enslaved thought, however, there is nothing to choose between the fake despair of a nondialectical critique on the one hand and the fake optimism of a plain and simple boosting of the system on the other.

197 THERE IS A SCHOOL of sociology, originating in the United States, which has begun to raise questions about the conditions of existence created by modern social development. But while this approach has been able to gather much empirical data, it is quite unable to grasp the true nature of its chosen object, because it cannot recognize the critique immanent to that object. The sincerely reformist orientation of this sociology has no criteria aside from morality, common sense and other such yardsticks – all utterly inadequate for dealing with the matter in hand. Because it is unaware of the negativity at the heart of its world, this mode of criticism is obliged to concentrate on describing a sort of surplus negativity that it views as a regrettable irritation, or an irrational parasitic infestation, affecting the *surface* of that world. An outraged goodwill of this kind, which even on its own terms can do nothing except put all the blame on the system's external consequences, can see itself as *critical* only by ignoring the essentially *apologetic* character of its assumptions and method.

198   PEOPLE WHO DENOUNCE incitements to wastefulness as absurd or dangerous in a society of economic abundance do not understand the purpose of waste. It is distinctly ungrateful of them to condemn, in the name of economic rationality, those faithful (albeit irrational) guardians without whom the power of that same economic rationality would collapse. Daniel Boorstin, for example, whose book *The Image* describes the spectacular consumption of commodities in America, never arrives at a concept of the spectacle because he mistakenly feels able to treat private life, like something he calls an "honest product," as quite independent of what he sees as a disastrous distortion or "exaggeration." What he fails to grasp is that the commodity form itself lays down laws whose "honest" application gives rise not only to private life as a distinct reality but also to that reality's subsequent conquest by the social consumption of images.

199   BOORSTIN TREATS the excesses of a world that has become alien to us as excesses alien to our world. The "normal" basis of social life to which he refers implicitly when he describes the superficial reign of images, in terms of psychological and moral judgments, as the product of "our ever more extravagant expectations," has no reality at all, however, either in his book or in the historical period in which he lives. Because the real human life that Boorstin evokes is located for him in the past — even in a past of religious passivity — he has no way of comprehending the true depth of society's dependence on images. The *truth* of that society is nothing less than its *negation*.

200 A SOCIOLOGY THAT believes it possible to isolate an industrial rationality, functioning on its own, from social life
as a whole, is liable likewise to view the technology of
reproduction and communication as independent of overall industrial development. Thus Boorstin accounts for the
situation he portrays in terms of an unfortunate and quasi-
serendipitous coming together of too vast a technology of
image-diffusion on the one hand, and, on the other, too
great an appetite for sensationalism on the part of today's
public. The spectacle, in this view, would have to be at-
tributed to man's "spectatorial" inclinations. Boorstin
cannot see that the proliferation of prefabricated "pseudo-
events" – which he deplores – flows from the simple fact
that, in face of the massive realities of present-day social
existence, individuals do not actually experience events.
Because history itself is the specter haunting modern society, pseudo-history has to be fabricated at every level of
the consumption of life; otherwise, the equilibrium of the
frozen time that presently holds sway could not be preserved.

201 THE CLAIM THAT a brief freeze in historical time is in fact
a definitive stability – such is, both consciously and unconsciously expressed, the undoubted basis of the current
tendency toward "structuralist" system building. The perspective adopted by the anti-historical thought of structuralism is that of the eternal presence of a system that
was never created and that will never disappear. This fan-
tasy of a preexisting unconscious structure's hegemony
over all social practice is illegitimately derived from lin-
guistic and anthropological structural models – even from

models of the functioning of capitalism – that are misapplied even in their original contexts; and the only reason why this has occurred is that an academic approach fit for complacent middle-range managers, a mode of thought completely anchored in an awestruck celebration of the existing system, crudely reduces all reality to the existence of that system.

202   IN SEEKING TO UNDERSTAND "structuralist" categories, it should always be borne in mind, as in the case of any historical social science, that categories express not only the forms but also the conditions of existence. Just as one does not judge a man's value according to the conception he has of himself, one cannot judge – or admire – this specific society by taking the discourse it addresses to itself as necessarily true. "One cannot judge such a period of transformation by its consciousness, but, on the contrary, this consciousness must be explained from the contradictions of material life." Structures are the progeny of the power that is in place. Structuralism is *a thought underwritten by the State*, a thought that conceives of the present conditions of spectacular "communication" as an absolute. Its fashion of studying the code of messages in itself is merely the product, and the acknowledgment, of a society where communication has the form of a cascade of hierarchical signals. Thus it is not structuralism that serves to prove the transhistorical validity of the society of the spectacle; but, on the contrary, it is the society of the spectacle, imposing itself in its massive reality, that validates the chill dream of structuralism.

203   WITHOUT A DOUBT, the critical concept of the *spectacle* is susceptible of being turned into just another empty formula of sociologico-political rhetoric designed to explain and denounce everything *in the abstract* – so serving to buttress the spectacular system itself. For obviously no *idea* could transcend the spectacle that exists – it could only transcend ideas that exist about the spectacle. For the society of the spectacle to be effectively destroyed, what is needed are people setting a practical force in motion. A critical theory of the spectacle cannot be true unless it joins forces with the practical movement of negation within society; and this negation, which constitutes the resumption of revolutionary class struggle, cannot for its part achieve self-consciousness unless it develops the critique of the spectacle, a critique that embodies the theory of negation's real conditions – the practical conditions of present-day oppression – and that also, inversely, reveals the secret of negation's potential. Such a theory expects no miracles from the working class. It views the reformulation and satisfaction of proletarian demands as a long-term undertaking. To make an artificial distinction between theoretical and practical struggle – for, on the basis here defined, the very constitution and communication of a theory of this kind cannot be conceived independently of a *rigorous practice* – we may say with certainty that the obscure and difficult path of critical theory must also be the path of the practical movement that occurs at the level of society as a whole.

204   CRITICAL THEORY has to be communicated in its own language – the language of contradiction, dialectical in

form as well as in content: the language of the critique of the totality, of the critique of history. Not some "writing degree zero" — just the opposite. Not a negation of style, but the style of negation.

205   EVEN THE STYLE OF exposition of dialectical theory is a scandal and an abomination to the canons of the prevailing language, and to sensibilities molded by those canons, because it includes in its positive use of existing concepts a simultaneous recognition of their rediscovered fluidity, of their inevitable destruction.

206   THIS STYLE, which embodies its own critique, must express the mastery of the critique in hand over all its predecessors. The mode of exposition of dialectical theory will thus itself exemplify the negative spirit it contains. The truth, says Hegel, is not "detached...like a finished article from the instrument that shapes it." Such a theoretical consciousness of dialectical movement, which must itself bear the stamp of that movement, is manifested by the *reversal* of established relationships between concepts and by the diversion (or *détournement*) of all the attainments of earlier critical efforts. Thus the reversed genitive, as an expression of historical revolutions distilled into a form of thought, came to be considered the hallmark of Hegel's epigrammatic style. As a proponent of the replacement of subject by predicate, following Feuerbach's systematic practice of it, the young Marx achieved the most cogent use of this *insurrectional style*: thus the philosophy of poverty became the poverty of philosophy. The device

of *détournement* restores all their subversive qualities to past critical judgments that have congealed into respectable truths – or, in other words, that have been transformed into lies. Kierkegaard too made use of *détournement*, and offered his own pronouncement on the subject: "But how you twist and turn, so that, just as Saft always ended up in the pantry, you inevitably always manage to introduce some little word or phrase that is not your own, and which awakens disturbing recollections" (*Philosophical Fragments*). The defining characteristic of this use of *détournement* is the necessity for *distance* to be maintained toward whatever has been turned into an official verity. As Kierkegaard acknowledges in the same work, "One further remark I wish to make, however, with respect to your many animadversions, all pointing to my having introduced borrowed expressions in the course of my exposition. That such is the case I do not deny, nor will I now conceal from you that it was done purposely, and that in the next section of this piece, if I ever write such a section, it is my intention to call the whole by its right name, and to clothe the problem in its historical costume."

207 IDEAS IMPROVE. The meaning of words has a part in the improvement. Plagiarism is necessary. Progress demands it. Staying close to an author's phrasing, plagiarism exploits his expressions, erases false ideas, replaces them with correct ideas.

208 *Détournement* IS THE ANTITHESIS of quotation, of a theoretical authority invariably tainted if only because it has

become quotable, because it is now a fragment torn away from its context, from its own movement, and ultimately from the overall frame of reference of its period and from the precise option that it constituted within that framework. *Détournement*, by contrast, is the fluid language of anti-ideology. It occurs within a type of communication aware of its inability to enshrine any inherent and definitive certainty. This language is inaccessible in the highest degree to confirmation by any earlier or supra-critical reference point. On the contrary, its internal coherence and its adequacy in respect of the practically possible are what validate the ancient kernel of truth that it restores. *Détournement* founds its cause on nothing but its own truth as critique at work in the present.

209 WHATEVER IS EXPLICITLY presented as *détournement* within formulated theory serves to deny any durable autonomous existence to the sphere of theory merely formulated. The fact that the violence of *détournement* itself mobilizes an action capable of disturbing or overthrowing any existing order is a reminder that the existence of the theoretical domain is nothing in itself, that it can only come to self-knowledge in conjunction with historical action, and that it can only be truly faithful by virtue of history's corrective judgment upon it.

210 ONLY THE REAL negation of culture can inherit culture's meaning. Such negation can no longer remain *cultural*. It is what remains, in some manner, at the level of culture — but it has a quite different sense.

211   IN THE LANGUAGE of contradiction, the critique of culture manifests itself as *unified*: unified in that it dominates
the whole of culture — culture as knowledge as well as culture as poetry; unified, too, in that it is no longer separa-
ble from the critique of the social totality. It is this unified
theoretical critique that goes alone to its rendezvous with
a *unified social practice*.

IX

Ideology In Material Form

Self-consciousness exists in itself and for itself, in that, and by the fact that it exists for another self-consciousness; that is to say, it is only by being acknowledged or "recognized."

— Hegel, *The Phenomenology of Mind*

212 IDEOLOGY IS THE *foundation* of the thought of a class society within the conflictual course of history. Ideological entities have never been mere fictions — rather, they are a distorted consciousness of reality, and, as such, real factors retroactively producing real distorting effects; which is all the more reason why that *materialization* of ideology, in the form of the spectacle, which is precipitated by the concrete success of an autonomous economic system of production, results in the virtual identification with social reality itself of an ideology that manages to remold the whole of the real to its own specifications.

213 ONCE IDEOLOGY, which is the *abstract* will to universality and the illusion thereof, finds itself legitimated in modern society by universal abstraction and by the effective dictatorship of illusion, then it is no longer the voluntaristic struggle of the fragmentary, but rather its triumph. The claims of ideology now take on a sort of flat, positivistic exactness: ideology is no longer a historical choice, but simply an assertion of the obvious. *Names* of particular ideologies have vanished. The portion of properly ideological labor serving the system may no longer be conceived of other than in terms of an "epistemological base" supposedly transcending all specific ideological phenomena. Ideology in material form is itself without a name, just as it is without a formulable historical agenda. Which is another way of saying that the history of ideologies, plural, is over.

214 IDEOLOGY, WHOSE WHOLE internal logic led toward what Mannheim calls "total ideology" — the despotism of a

fragment imposing itself as the pseudo-knowledge of a frozen *whole*, as a *totalitarian* worldview — has now fulfilled itself in the immobilized spectacle of non-history. Its fulfillment is also its dissolution into society as a whole. Come the *practical dissolution* of that society itself, ideology — the *last unreason* standing in the way of historical life — must likewise disappear.

215   THE SPECTACLE IS the acme of ideology, for in its full flower it exposes and manifests the essence of all ideological systems: the impoverishment, enslavement and negation of real life. Materially, the spectacle is "the expression of estrangement, of alienation between man and man." The "new potentiality of fraud" concentrated within it has its basis in that form of production whereby "with the mass of objects grows the mass of alien powers to which man is subjected." This is the supreme stage of an expansion that has turned need against life. "The need for money is for that reason the real need created by the modern economic system, and the only need it creates" (*Economic and Philosophical Manuscripts*). The principle which Hegel enunciated in the *Jenenser Realphilosophie* as that of money — "the life, moving of itself, of that which is dead" — has now been extended by the spectacle to the entirety of social life.

216   IN CONTRAST TO the project outlined in the *Theses on Feuerbach* — the realization of philosophy in a praxis transcending the opposition between idealism and materialism — the spectacle preserves the ideological features of both materialism and idealism, imposing them in the

pseudo-concreteness of its universe. The contemplative aspect of the old materialism, which conceives of the world as representation, not as activity – and which in the last reckoning idealizes matter – has found fulfillment in the spectacle, where concrete things are automatically masters of social life. Correlatively, idealism's *imaginary activity* likewise finds its fulfillment in the spectacle, this through the technical mediation of signs and signals – which in the last reckoning endow an abstract ideal with material form.

217 THE PARALLEL BETWEEN ideology and schizophrenia drawn by Joseph Gabel in his *False Consciousness* should be seen in the context of this economic process of materialization of ideology. What ideology already was, society has now become. A blocked practice and its corollary, an antidialectical false consciousness, are imposed at every moment on an everyday life in thrall to the spectacle – an everyday life that should be understood as the systematic organization of a breakdown in the faculty of encounter, and the replacement of that faculty by a *social hallucination*: a false consciousness of encounter, or an "illusion of encounter." In a society where no one is any longer recognizable by anyone else, each individual is necessarily unable to recognize his own reality. Here ideology is at home; here separation has built its world.

218 "IN CLINICAL PICTURES of schizophrenia," according to Gabel, "a degradation of the dialectic of the totality (of which dissociation is the extreme form) and a degradation

in the dialectic of becoming (of which catatonia is the extreme form) seem to be intimately interwoven." Imprisoned in a flat universe bounded on all sides by the spectacle's *screen*, the consciousness of the spectator has only figmentary interlocutors which subject it to a one-way discourse on their commodities and the politics of those commodities. The sole mirror of this consciousness is the spectacle in all its breadth, where what is staged is a false way out of a generalized autism.

219   THE SPECTACLE ERASES the dividing line between self and world, in that the self, under siege by the presence/absence of the world, is eventually overwhelmed; it likewise erases the dividing line between true and false, repressing all directly lived truth beneath the *real presence* of the falsehood maintained by the organization of appearances. The individual, though condemned to the passive acceptance of an alien everyday reality, is thus driven into a form of madness in which, by resorting to magical devices, he entertains the illusion that he is reacting to this fate. The recognition and consumption of commodities are at the core of this pseudo-response to a communication to which no response is possible. The need to imitate that the consumer experiences is indeed a truly infantile need, one determined by every aspect of his fundamental dispossession. In terms used by Gabel to describe quite another level of pathology, "the abnormal need for representation here compensates for a torturing feeling of being at the margin of existence."

220 WHEREAS THE LOGIC of false consciousness cannot accede to any genuine self-knowledge, the quest for the critical truth of the spectacle must also be a true critique. This quest calls for commitment to a practical struggle alongside the spectacle's irreconcilable enemies, as well as a readiness to withhold commitment where those enemies are not active. By eagerly embracing the machinations of reformism or making common cause with pseudo-revolutionary dregs, those driven by the abstract wish for immediate efficacity obey only the laws of the dominant forms of thought, and adopt the exclusive viewpoint of *actuality*. In this way delusion is able to reemerge within the camp of its erstwhile opponents. The fact is that a critique capable of surpassing the spectacle must *know how to bide its time.*

221 SELF-EMANCIPATION in our time is emancipation from the material bases of an inverted truth. This "historic mission to establish truth in the world" can be carried out neither by the isolated individual nor by atomized and manipulated masses, but — only and always — by that class which is able to effect the dissolution of all classes, subjecting all power to the disalienating form of a realized democracy — to councils in which practical theory exercises control over itself and surveys its own action. It cannot be carried out, in other words, until individuals are "directly bound to universal history"; until dialogue has taken up arms to impose its own conditions upon the world.

This edition designed by Bruce Mau
with Greg Van Alstyne
Type composed by Archetype
Printed and bound Smythe-sewn by Maple-Vail
using Sebago acid-free paper